Sowing Unrest

tranzit.cz

Matter of Art

Constitutions I

Galina Rymbu
2023

1.
all lives desire.
    all lives desire to know.
        a desiring life for all.

2.
life desires in all languages.
not in a single one.

even before form there is also life.

3.
both the human-plant, and the
animal-mushroom, and the complex
ant, and the three-hearted octopus,
and the changeful salamander, and
the seal, and the communicating
whale—*life defeats the apparatus
of capture.*

4.
what we can know must not be sold.
knowledge is for free.
labor is secret.

5.
if a home is beds of blood,
then the rest and shelter in it is
horror.

6.
I
and
you
are the institute of earth-states.

7.
everyone will create their life
as they desire.
everyone will create the
institute of earth-states.

8.
to the friend, a friend.
everything is for one another.

9.
all species are companions. *new relatives.* their meeting is a world without weapons.

10.
the labor of others cannot be sold. only free circulation of things and beings, as they desire.

resources belong to all and circulate, distributing themselves as needed. all needs are accounted for. across the earth—the movement of lovers, states of labor defined by desire, tenderness, knowledge.

11.
nothing can be done, created against desire.

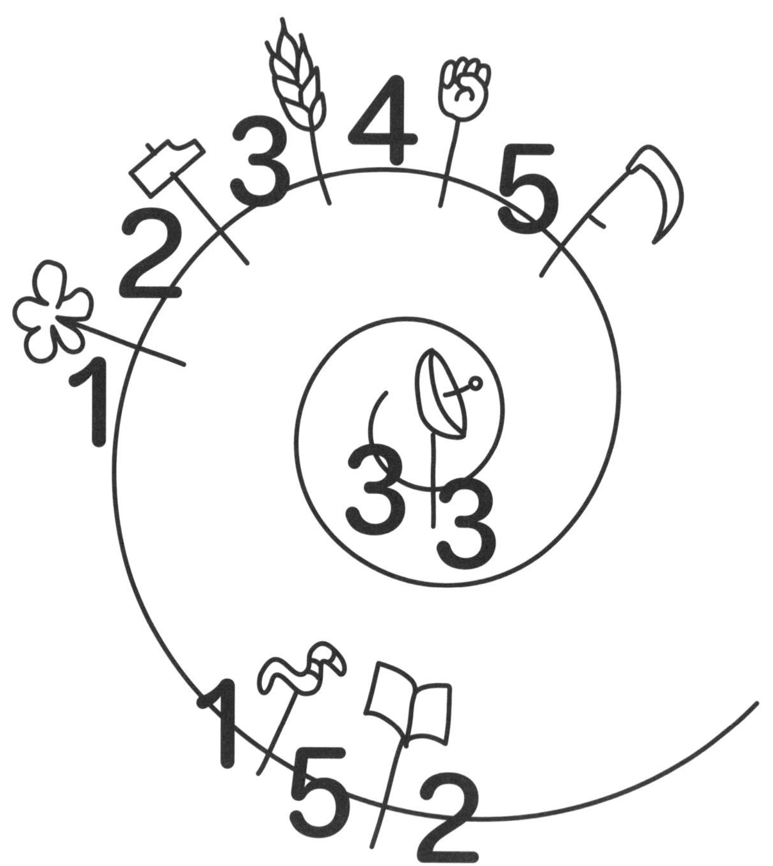
1 2 3 4 5
1 5 2
3 3

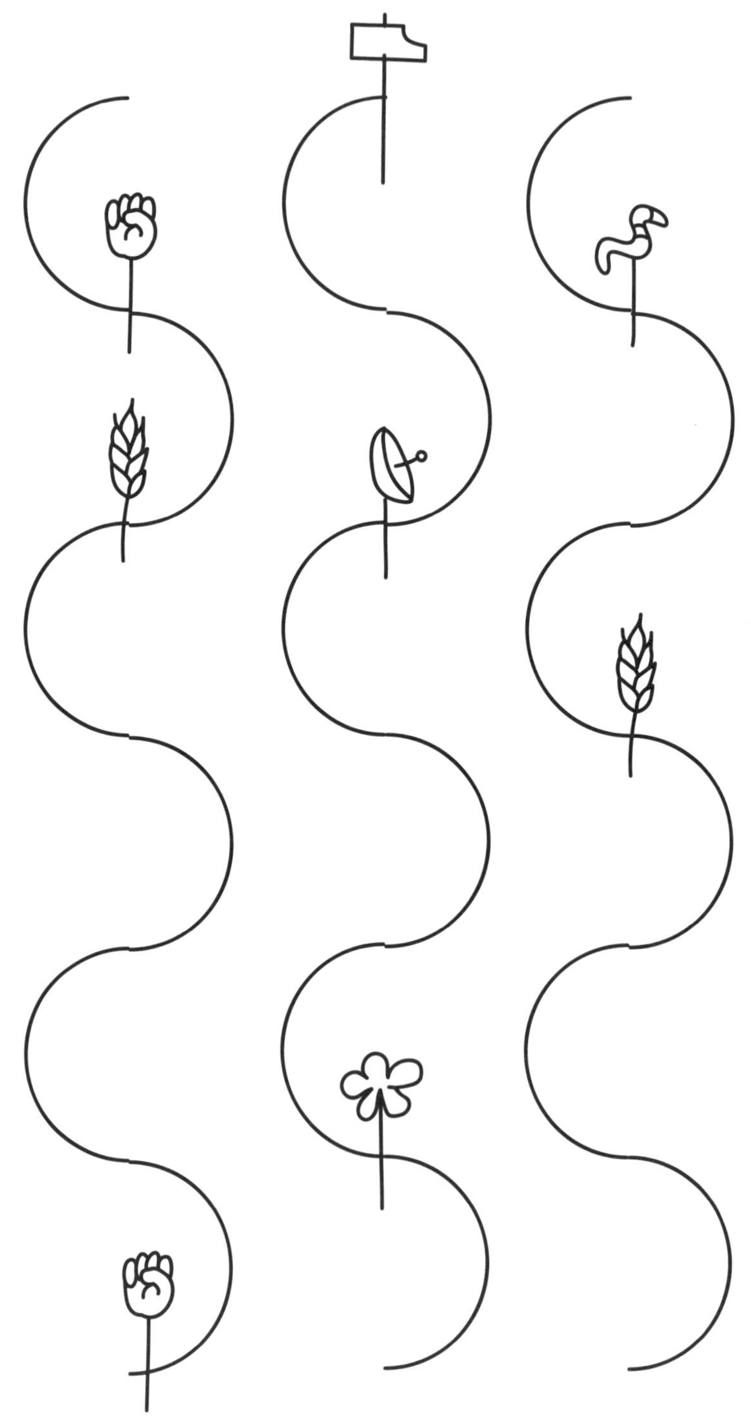

Sowing Unrest

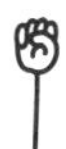

An introduction in conversation

Aleksei Borisionok .... AB
and Katalin Erdődi .... KE

Since the winter of 2022, we have been working together on unfolding a dialogue between our curatorial interests that took shape in the form of the biennale exhibition and the accompanying reader *Sowing Unrest* that you now have before you. Being in conversation has defined our collaboration, so we decided to introduce the reader in this form, to open up our exchange, share our research, while also introducing you to our invited contributors.

KE My interest in the rural, in particular rural change, stems from my personal history. My father comes from a small village in eastern Hungary and my grandparents worked the land as peasants, in a cooperative and on their household farm. Their sons both left the village for the city and my father even went to university, so my family's story is one of rural-to-urban migration and social mobility, which is quite typical of the socialist era. When I was growing up, we visited my grandparents every two weeks and I saw how their lives were transformed by the transition in the early '90s—how they tried to adapt to the free market, the challenges

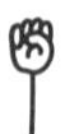

and opportunities they faced. I remember being intrigued by events such as the rise of cucumber farming in the region. Cucumbers sold at a very good price, so everybody started growing them—I remember the hot summer days spent picking and sorting them into categories. In the end, too many cucumbers were produced and the prices fell, you could hardly sell them anymore. The free market was totally unpredictable for people who were used to the planned economy and stable prices of socialism. There was a lot of stress and worry; it was unclear as to whether small farmers like my grandparents could survive, not to mention thrive. The apples they harvested in the fall often still waited in storage, unsold until the spring. At university, a friend wrote his PhD in sociology about rural development, analyzing this particular case of cucumber farming in my family's region from the perspective of innovators and imitators. It was then that I fitted my personal experience into a larger narrative of structural change.

In the reader, Polish anthropologist Tomasz Rakowski deals with this "quiet history" of the countryside. He shows how these situated experiences of rural change are key to understanding social change at large. His essay challenges the continuity of cultural stereotypes that attribute backwardness and passivity to rural people and calls for a decolonization of our thinking in this regard. This is also at the heart of my curatorial approach.[1] I find it especially important that Tomasz doesn't propose decolonization in a revisionist manner, as a mere revival of rural culture, but understands it as a "turn to freedom"—a freedom from cultural constraints.

1
For more about my curatorial trajectory and approach, see: Katalin Erdődi, "Songs of Resilience and Rural Counterpublics," Journal for Social Vision, accessed April 18, 2024, https://www.journalforsocialvision.org/post/land-of-songs.

AB My interest in workers' movements also comes from my family. My mother has worked in the trade unions federation of Belarus for three decades. Together with her, and through her work, we have been witnessing the complete degradation of workers' autonomy and the instrumentalization of the unions by state ideology. At the same time, both of us were surprised by the tremendous energy that was released by the social uprising in Belarus in 2020. Prefigurative forms of political organizing emerged during that summer and sparked networks of self-organization, striking and labor unrest, marches of all kinds of social and professional groups: from students, pensioners and people with disabilities to queer columns. We wondered: how is this possible? I assume the answer lies in many places—even such authoritarian bodies as official trade unions could bring people together, and they were able to subvert their form and use it for their true purpose—for the political and economic struggle. In many other liberal democratic countries—such as Poland or the Czech Republic—tendencies of neoliberal deregulation also put workers' organization and unions and other forms of cooperativism at a disadvantage. Besides that, the changing character of work itself—for example de-industrialization, the rise of outsourced labor, precarity—has affected forms of effective struggle in the field of labor.

My curatorial research attempted to follow these tendencies, and together with artistic contributions to capture the changing landscape of work regimes, organized and spontaneous forms of labor unrest in post-socialist contexts and beyond. The visual contribution by the eeefff group, based on their ongoing practice of *The School of Algorithmic Solidarity* derived from sophisticated ways of organizing using digital tools, navigates us through struggles in the field of computation and hacking. In their material analysis of digital infrastructures, the rural-urban divide becomes visible in unexpected ways—for example, how data centers and Amazon warehouses are being erected in the countryside, or how internet cables are becoming part of the landscape.

KE The ongoing transformation of rural landscapes with data centers and logistics parks as you mentioned, but also solar fields and wind turbines, is a burning issue across rural areas in Europe. It touches on the politics of land use and ownership, but also on the changing value of agricultural land—what good is fertile soil if you can no longer make a living from producing good-quality food on a small scale? Farmlands are transformed into logistics or energy landscapes, and once this happens there is no way back, the soil is contaminated by this new use. Use and uselessness have a very dynamic relationship within rural contexts. In her visual contribution, the artist and sheep farmer Orla Barry shares shearling felts that she created from wool she couldn't sell—its value was so low that it would not even cover the labor costs of the shearer. She juxtaposes the felts with a conversation she had with a wool merchant, with whom they trace how wool, such a beautiful and highly valued material, became a worthless by-product, and how the merchant's wool shed was turned into a warehouse for ready-to-assemble furniture.

Neoliberal platform capitalism and new energy infrastructures are not the only forces transforming rural landscapes. In her poetic text, "When the Sun Sets East," the artist and writer Kateryna Aliinyk confronts the transformation of her native landscape in Ukraine's Donbas region through war. Kateryna reminds us that our attachment to a place, to a land, is both embodied and imagined. Landscapes are formed by complex human and non-human relations—they are not mere backdrops, but full-fledged protagonists of rural realities and imaginaries.

They bear witness to manifold processes of change, they are living archives. But how do we access the stories they have to tell, how can we engage with and narrate these human and non-human entanglements?

When researching rural change I am often guided by the feminist anthropologist Anna Tsing, who argues that "to listen to and tell a rush of stories is a method" and "to learn anything we must revitalize the arts of noticing and include ethnography and natural history."[2] This "art of noticing" resonates with Orla's and Kateryna's approach, but also with Tomasz Rakowski's contribution; they all find unique ways—through art or research—to tell such a rush of stories. What archives, what rush of stories are relevant for your research?

AB The rush of stories I am trying to excavate in my work comes from the histories of (post-)socialism, in connection with the contradictory heritage of emancipation and oppression. These stories are mostly neglected or instrumentalized by state ideologies; however, we can find their traces in some museums and archives, orally shared knowledge or embodied experience. For me, interest in museums is not merely about the past—it is a question of how to assemble our contradictory heritage and use it critically for our needs today. This is why I find many post-socialist museums interesting, because after the collapse of state socialisms they become fragmented, their displays have ruptures. If a museum is closed, unavailable or simply non-existent, or if we don't agree with its official history of labor, gender, class and racial configurations, perhaps it makes sense to fabulate museums that would

2
Anna Lowenhaupt Tsing, *The Mushroom at the End of the World: On the Possibility of Life in Capitalist Ruins* (Princeton: Princeton University Press, 2017), 37.

reflect our understanding of the history and materiality of labor, a queer linearity of time, to grasp contradictions and respect various types of labor—also that which is invisible. Galina Rymbu in her poem "[only our neighborhood had so many factories]"–presented in the reader–refers to post-socialism as a straight line of history that comes to an end. She writes about her childhood experience of growing up in an industrial city with many factories that have been privatized and destroyed, with the result that people have been forced to think of different ways of living and surviving. She says that even the language which we use to speak about work is being eroded.

My family experience also formed the impulse for my interest in the museums of workers movements. Unlike most countries with the experience of state socialism, where workers', revolutionary or party museums were closed in the 1990s, Minsk still has one. However, believe it or not, I have not been able to visit it for various reasons.[3] At the same time, it motivated me to think about what the museum of workers' movements could be. This is why I took an interest in other museums during our research—such as the Museum of the Cooperative Association, a tiny and well-hidden museum in the center of Prague that tells the history of cooperative movements in the region, or the Lidice Art Collection with its unique art collection based on the principle of solidarity.

3
I described this experience in the following essay: Aleksei Borisionok, "The Secret Museum of the Workers Movement," *Lulu-journal*, no. 9 (February 2021): https://www.luleabiennial.se/en/journalen/nr-9/the-secret-museum-of-the-workers-movement.

4
The Museum of Karl Marx was established in 1960 and closed down in 1989. See: "Muzeum Karla Marxe, Karlovy Vary," Mapa Muzea dělnického hnutí v 21. století, accessed April 18, 2024, https://mdh.dejepis21.cz/mapa/muzea-a-pamatniky-revolucniho-hnuti/detail/?objectId=12.

Also, my research during the work on the Matter of Art Biennale caused me to investigate the history of the Museum of Karl Marx in Karlovy Vary.[4] Because Marx traveled there several times to improve his health as an old and sick man, the socialist government of Czechoslovakia decided to celebrate his visits and founded the exhibition in 1960. For me this historical fact articulated various ideas about workers' agency, labor and leisure, the political economy of health, production traumas and regeneration. At the same time, the writing of Kateřina Kolářová on post-socialism was essential and inspiring. She approaches this notion through the concept of inarticulate post-socialist crip, questioning the ways in which health and able-bodiedness were instrumental during the times of neoliberal transition. In the reader we are publishing a fragment of her forthcoming book, where she develops this argument relating to controversial histories of precarity, in which hardship and perseverance such as disability, sickness and homelessness were framed within the ideologies of cruel optimism.

KE Speaking of museums, it is important to talk about representation and self-representation, and whether the social groups these museums are dedicated to actually feel represented by them. Do these institutions support or rather hinder their emancipatory struggles? In our conversation with Ramona Duminicioiu, Fernando García-Dory, Alex Toshkov and Tomáš Uhnák, we talked about "rural internationalism" and the current need for stronger, more transnational self-organizing of peasant movements in the region. Through my research for the biennale, I learned that between the two World Wars Czechoslovakia co-founded the Green International with Bulgaria and Yugoslavia—a unique "rural international" initiated by East European agrarian governments—with Prague as the headquarters of its International Agrarian Bureau.[5] The Green International was relatively short-lived and quickly forgotten, even its archives disappeared. This prompted me to think about how we can remember and learn from such past struggles, but also about the ways in which transnational organizing is relevant for *the region today.* La Via Campesina [The Peasant Way] is one of the largest radical rural social movements globally, but it hardly has any active members in Eastern Europe, except for in Romania. In the conversation, but also in his new work for the biennale, the artist and researcher Tomáš Uhnák provocatively asks: who and where are the peasants in Czechia today? What kind of political subjectivity do small farmers and agricultural workers (mostly migrant seasonal workers) have and what can unite them in their struggles against exploitation, precarity and the toxic expansion of agri-business and industrial farming?

I am interested in foregrounding these emancipatory struggles, especially focusing on the post-socialist transformations within the region. Cooperation, solidarity and mutual aid are very much embedded in rural life, as people would not be able to survive otherwise—they exchange work and resources, they rely on one another, but this is done in predominantly informal, self-organized and thus largely invisible ways. I strive to approach the rural as a subaltern counterpublic—drawing on Nancy Fraser's feminist critique[6] of Jürgen Habermas's bourgeois public sphere—because I see it as an underrepresented and marginalized public sphere.

5

Read more about the Green International in: Alex Toshkov, *Agrarianism as Modernity in 20th-Century Europe: The Golden Age of the Peasantry* (London: Bloomsbury Academic, 2019).

6

Nancy Fraser, "Rethinking the Public Sphere: A Contribution to the Critique of Actually Existing Democracy," *Social Text*, no. 25/26 (1990): 56–80, https://doi.org/10.2307/466240.

AB The gesture of making public is relevant here: how do we bring to light and articulate these informal political practices and knowledges so that we can not only learn about but also learn from the rural? During our work on the biennale, the full-scale imperialist war against Ukraine, the devastation of Gaza in Palestine, as well as other humanitarian crises have aggravated existing urgencies—the destruction of land, museums and archives, imminent and slow ecological violence and pollution, and colonial dispossession. The character of Russian imperialism—which unfortunately often is not recognized by the Western left and Global South—forces us to think about the notion of solidarity and its limitations.

The conversation about care, unionization and labor unrest between Marta Romankiv, Olia Sosnovskaya and Maja Vusilović discusses possible forms of solidarity in the care work sector, as well as frameworks of post-socialisms and limitations of solidarity in the fields where the hypervisible can become invisible. I believe that our project in general—both the exhibition and the reader—helps to excavate various forms of solidarity and mutual aid, from various historical contexts and geographies which have often failed. Despite this failure, there are certain energies recovered that help us question the linearity of time and the instrumentalization of history and redefine the ways of struggling against contemporary forms of extractivism, imperialism and fascism. In the publication, we decided to focus on the practice of the artist Kateryna Lysovenko, who is deeply engaged with understanding the backgrounds of political violence, destruction as well as resilience. For her, the landscape and the museum becomes an environment that hosts various human and non-human subjects, who are able to survive imperialist destruction, regenerate and be together.

AB, KE Surviving and regenerating together were important impulses with regard to why we chose grafting as our curatorial method, as a means of joining our curatorial interests together, both in the exhibition and in the reader.

Inspired by the technique of grafting, we ask ourselves how we can graft solidarities across the rural-urban divide. Instead of letting our differences separate us, how can we create new alliances and grow stronger together? This is exactly what grafting does. It is a technique used in agriculture and medicine to join different plant parts or animal or human tissues so that they can grow together and become stronger.

Grafting can also be understood as a way of thinking that is not isolated and individual, but collective and unexpected. The work of the philosopher Michael Marder was particularly important to us in this regard. In his book *Grafts: Writings on Plants*, he asks: "How is it possible for two kinds of thinking to blossom or come to fruition together, on the same trunk/body/corpus? [...] *Grafts* unfolds (and grafts unfold) within the in-between space where previously unimagined forms of thinking eventually come to life."[7]

Grafting shows us the possibility for transformation in surprising and unexpected ways, which are not restricted to fixed identities—"quiet rebellion against the strictures of identity."[8] We can initiate grafting, but we cannot control whether it succeeds or fails.

The notion of grafting is also present in the visual contribution by Tamás Kaszás, who combines the teachings of permaculture with the language of socialist agricultural propaganda posters in order to create different speculative visions of the

7 Michael Marder, *Grafts: Writings on Plants* (Minneapolis: Univocal, 2016), 17–18.

8 Ibid., 15.

future in his graphic works. The question of possible, more emancipatory, livable and just futures has been central for both of us, but we also find it important to address and acknowledge the immediate present. The reader opens with the poem "Constitutions I" by Galina Rymbu, in which the poet formulates the basic conditions for living in doomed times, a common ground which can enable us to resist the horror of the present day.

We invite you to engage with this reader as a companion and extension to the biennale exhibition, in which we have grafted multiple texts and conversations to further elaborate questions about current struggles across the rural–urban divide, forms of unrest and solidarity, poetic interpretations of changing regimes of living, working and resting.

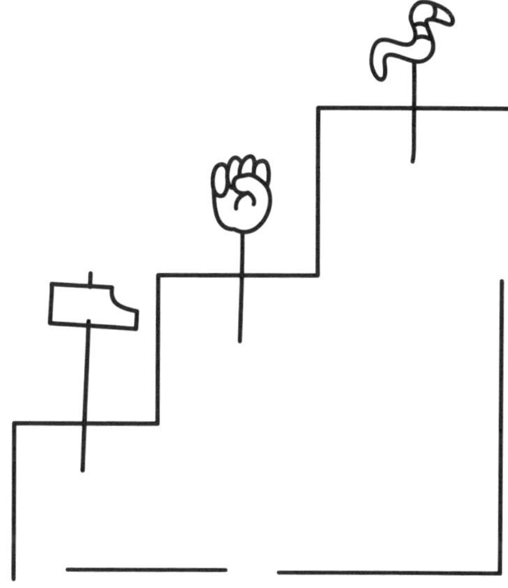

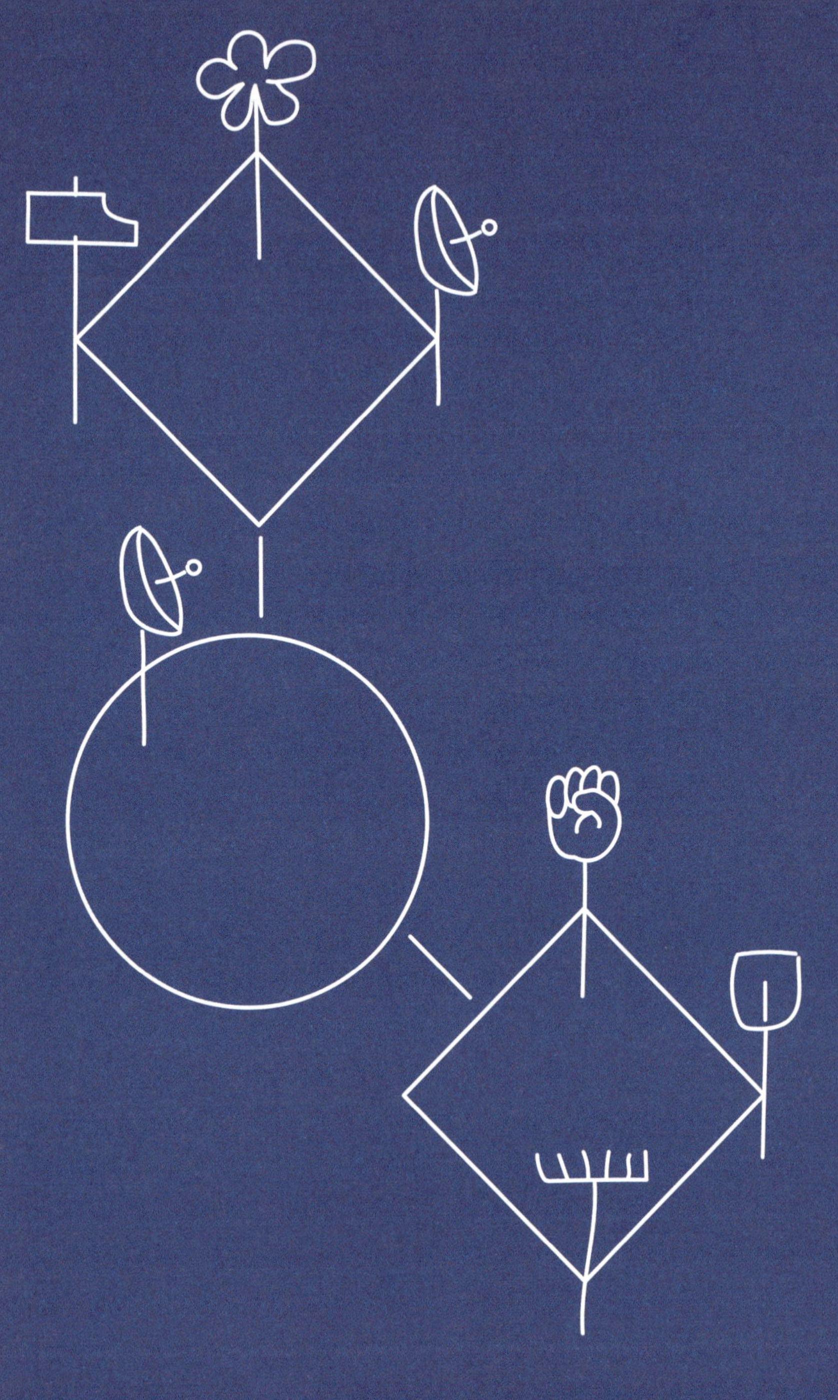

The School of Algorithmic Solidarity

eeefff

‘The school of algorithmic solidarity’ proposes to clash together two contradictory vectors: algorithms and solidarities, attempting for not-solvable, provocative, going-to-mad, togetherness / open-ended situation / affective temporary training zone.

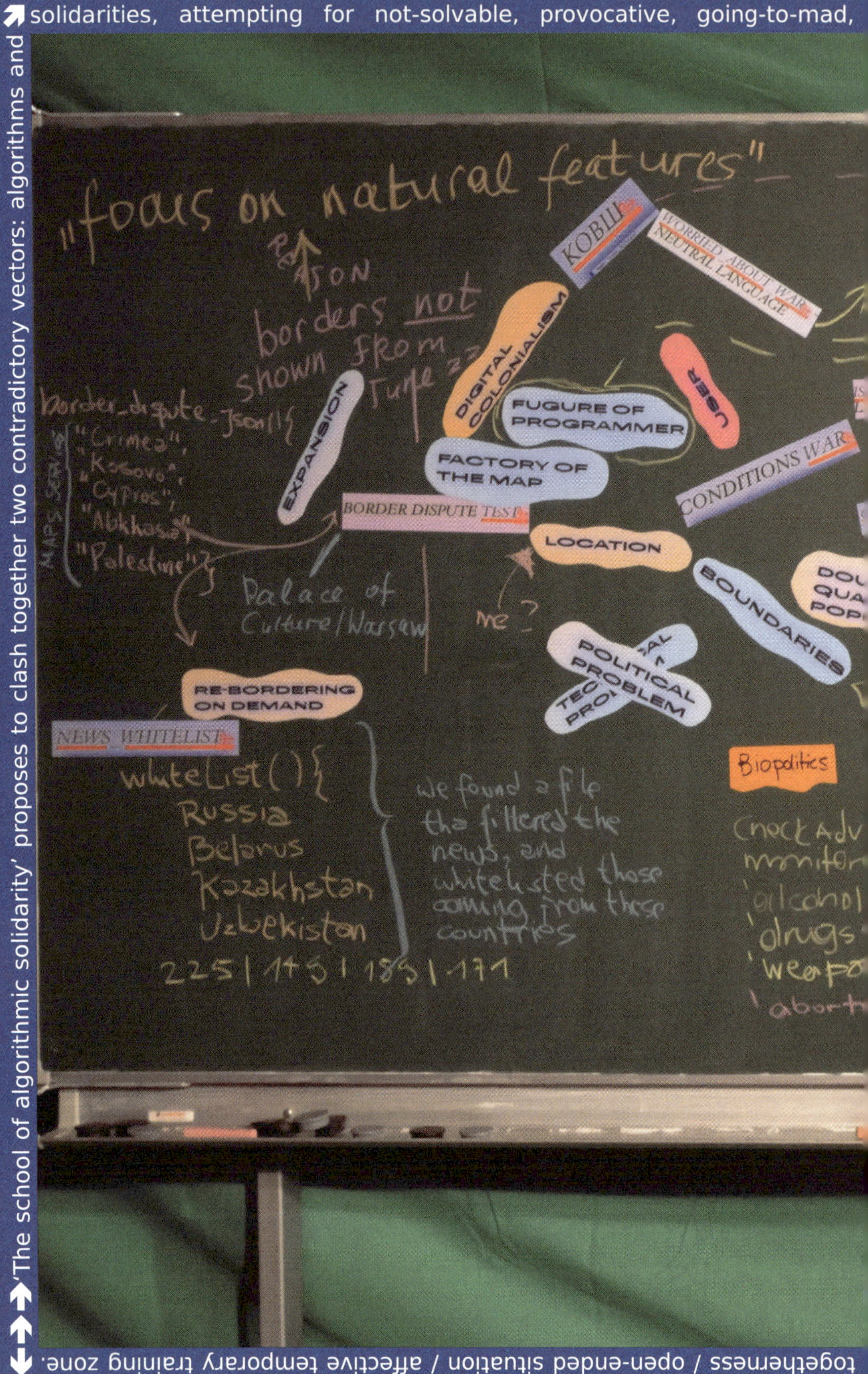

having-no-answer, inventory, imaginative. Specifically looking into infrastructural time, algorithmic abstractions and bodies. By form, it can be a collective experience / radical pedagogy practice / walk to the specific location / LARP protocol / digital

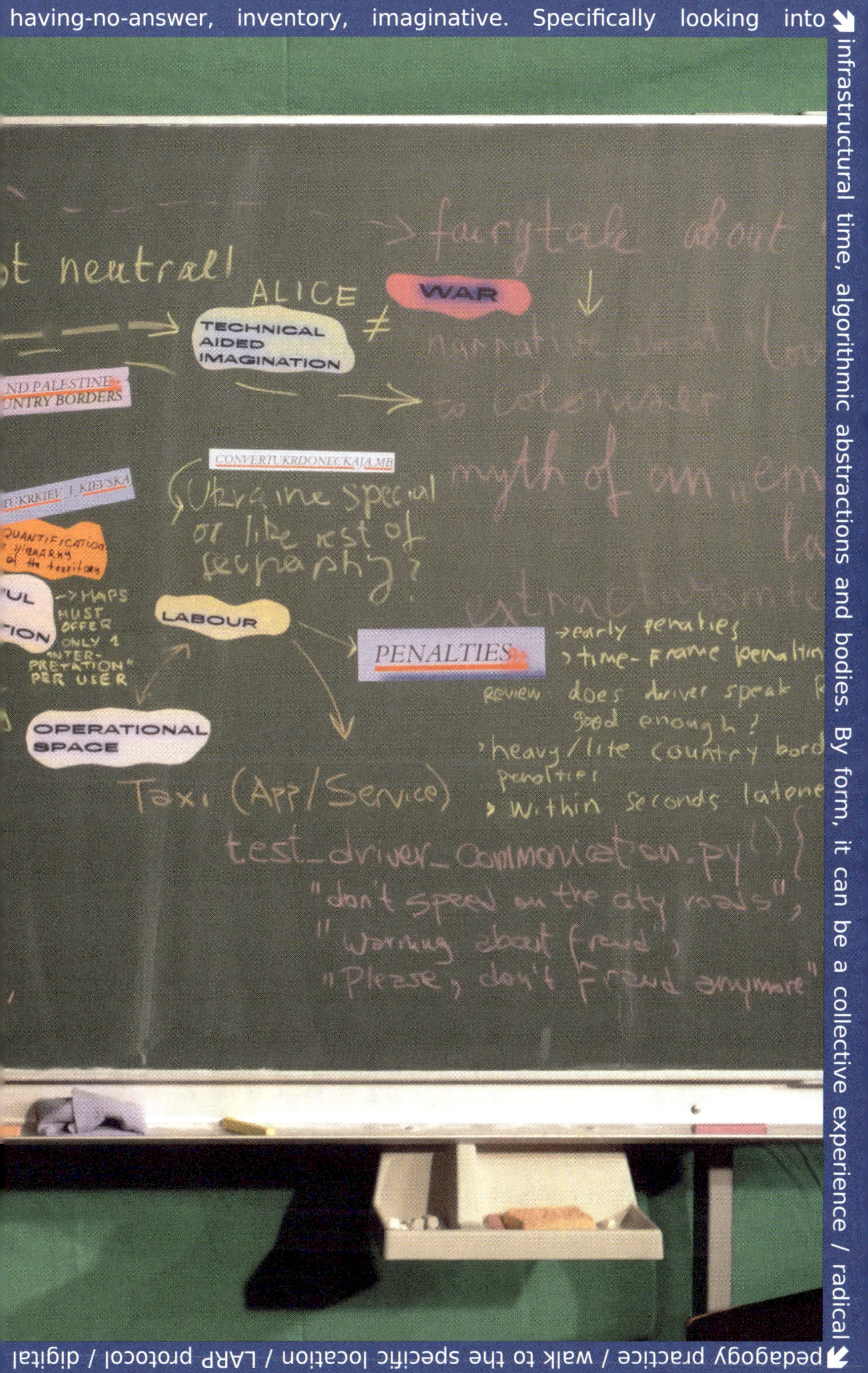

Each time one of the ????????????ions is raised that forms the logic and poetics of a session. The school operates spontaneously, without a permanent space or temporality, fictional connections (that by their affect can potentially become non-

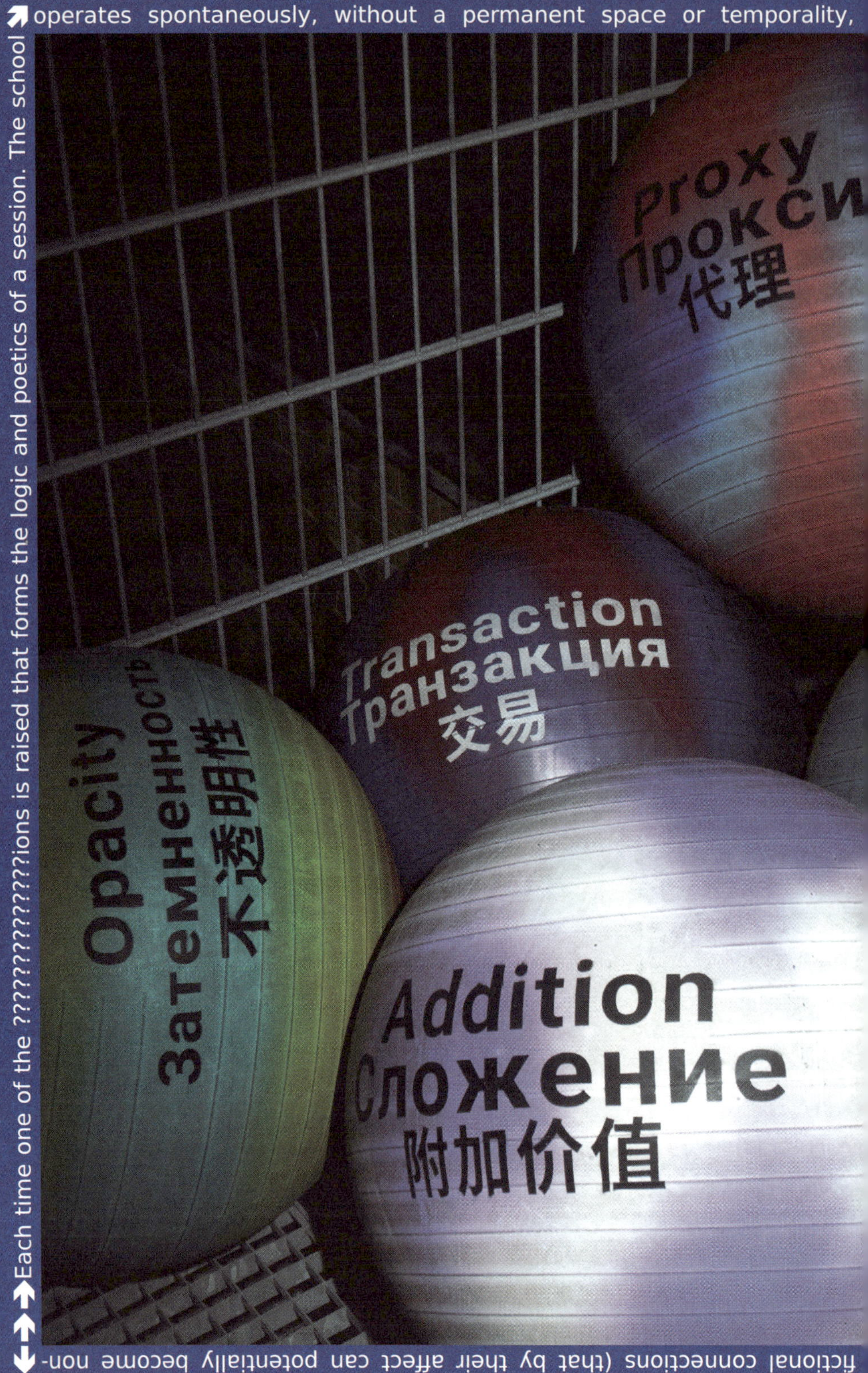

being unstable and fragile, occupying city holes for its actions, online spots for hacking their seemingly spotless interfaces, friendly initiatives' spaces, exhibitions and gardens. It is an

ABOUR INTERFACES

Let's play out division of labour game[2].

rt of your group pretends to be a "worker", another part — a nanager". Go to this website and make an account there according to ur role in this game.

[2] Our mission is to organize mutual aid, resources, and advocacy to improve conditions for all people using Amazon's Mechanical Turk (AMT) platform while striving to make this work a good job for all.

Find your position in this financial landscape. Share with others.

Search the words of your choice and discuss in the group the hierarchies of knowledge and power behind the dataset.

EXTRACTIVISM

To make this landscape more material look through one of the map of datacenters[11] or try to use something like google map.

- where are the most condensed areas? why?
- where is no data, or what places are not documented?
- how the appearance of such infrastructural object in one space can influence the urban tissue?
- where your data is stored? in which country, do you know?

...osed by ... computation

OMPAROLOGY

what this labour interface could say about generated pictures that were given to us?

TASETS

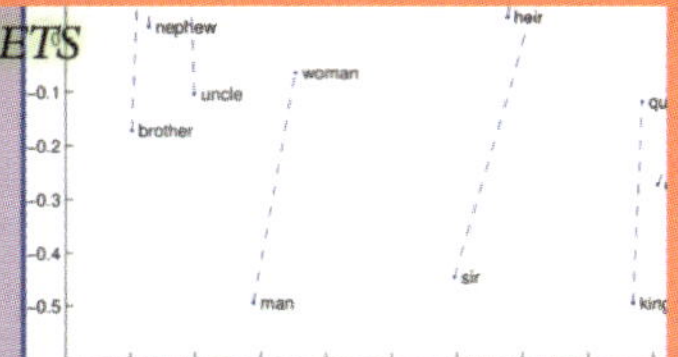

quantification: concepts converted into numbers

are some datasets[14] you can explore ack this. While going through them think about:

- what is quantified?
- what was calculated?
- what could not be calculated? if not so it is not a part of so called "AI"?
- who have made it? Was it paid work?
- who owned this data?

INTIMATE INTERFACE

- what the package of the device could say us?
- what is the size of the device?
- what is the material?
- how does it smell?
- how big are different parts?
- is there any sign that indicates its origin from where it comes? did you look inside?
- Is it specially designed part or standard?
- what kind of metrics and measurements you could apply to it?
- do you have similar device at your home? wanna disassemble it too?

attempt to gather a quickly-assembled community, temporary forum,

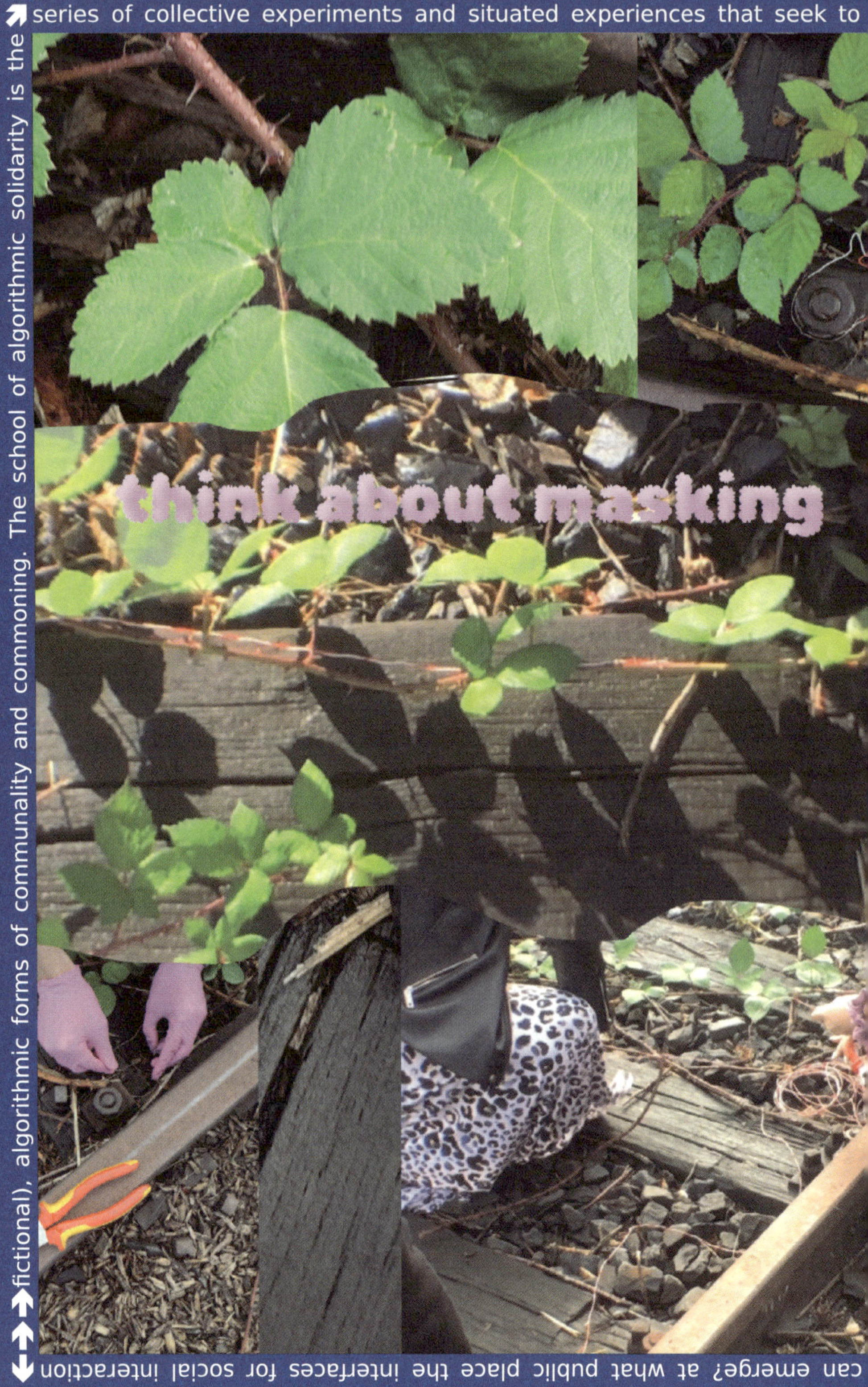

can emerge? at what public place the interfaces for social interaction

fictional), algorithmic forms of communality and commoning. The school of algorithmic solidarity is the

series of collective experiments and situated experiences that seek to answer the questions: can colonialism be encoded into algorithms? when the politics of the street intersects with the politics of digital materiality? can we redefine algorithmization in socio-political terms? what are new forms of digital communalization that

How many hours did you spend at ...g to feel ...e ...nfrastructure?

learning how

ready to taste real infrastructure

being awarded

protesting workers blocking the railway tracks

supply chains

slowing

15 years in prison for an infrastructure

wagon

symptom objects

cable

centr

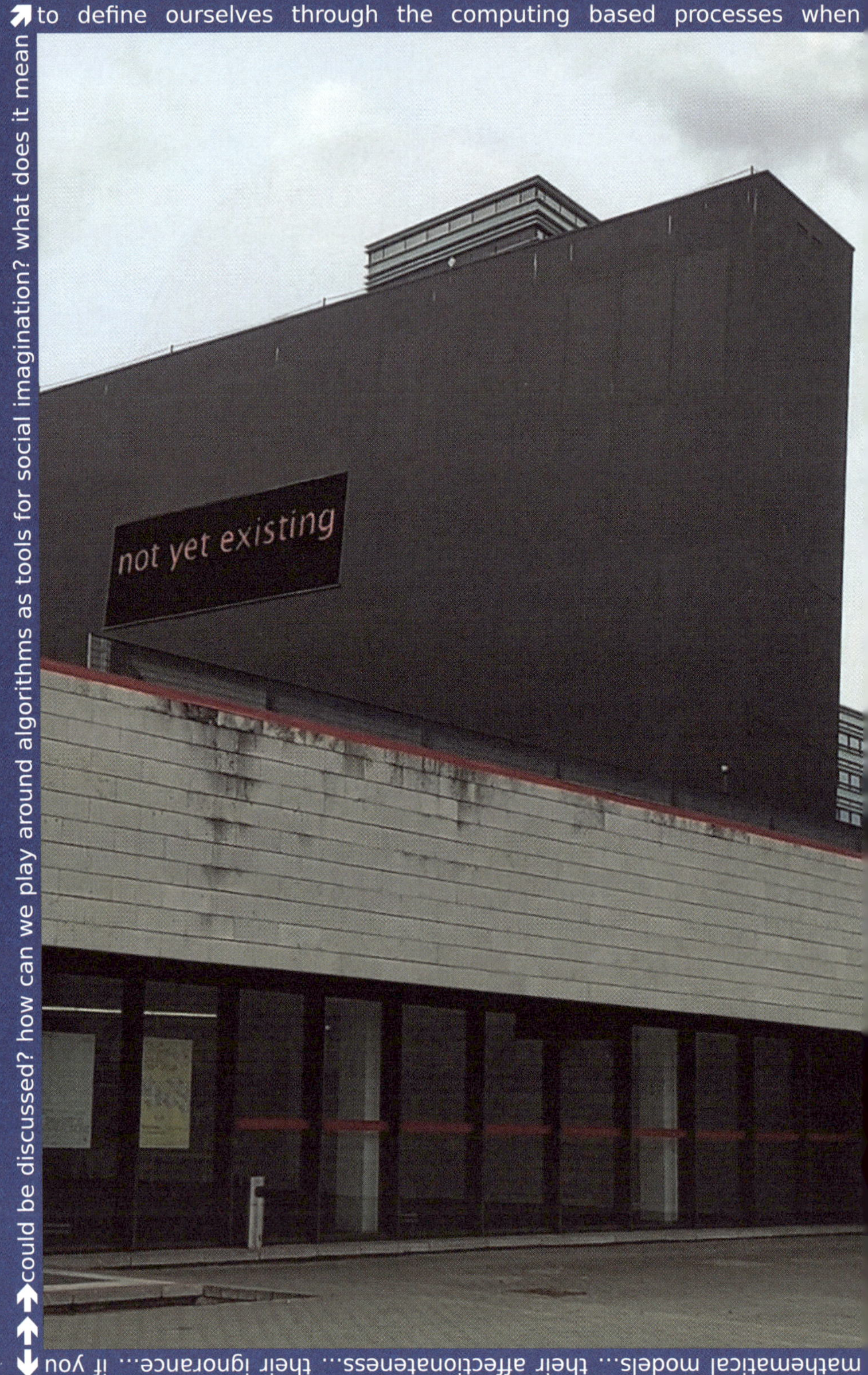

could be discussed? how can we play around algorithms as tools for social imagination? what does it mean to define ourselves through the computing based processes when mathematical models... their affectionateness... their ignorance... if you computing overlaps conventional cartographies? if we work from the network, we communicate using the network, why can't we use it as a tool for experimenting with new models of solidarity? please remember the last time when you felt the brutality of

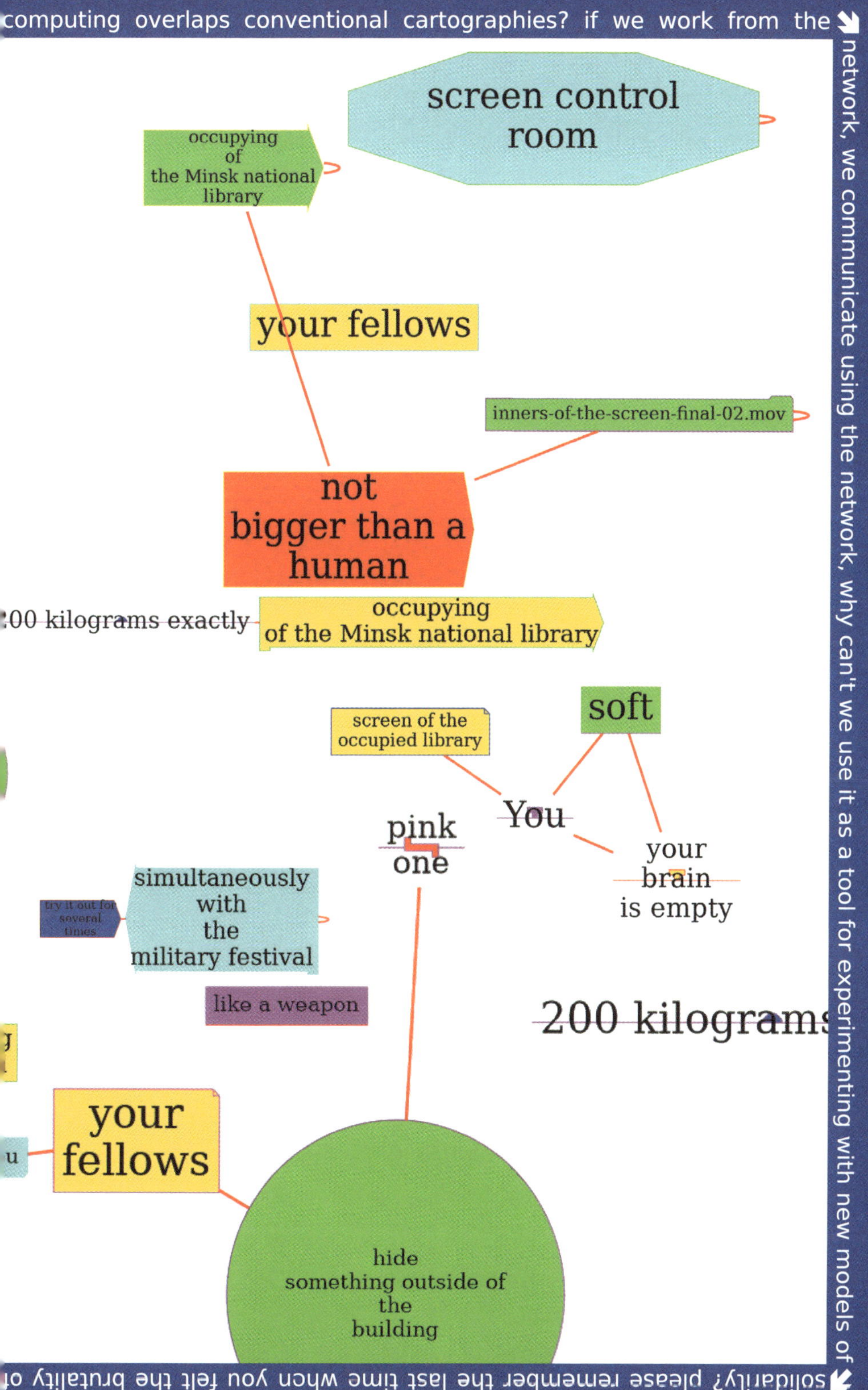

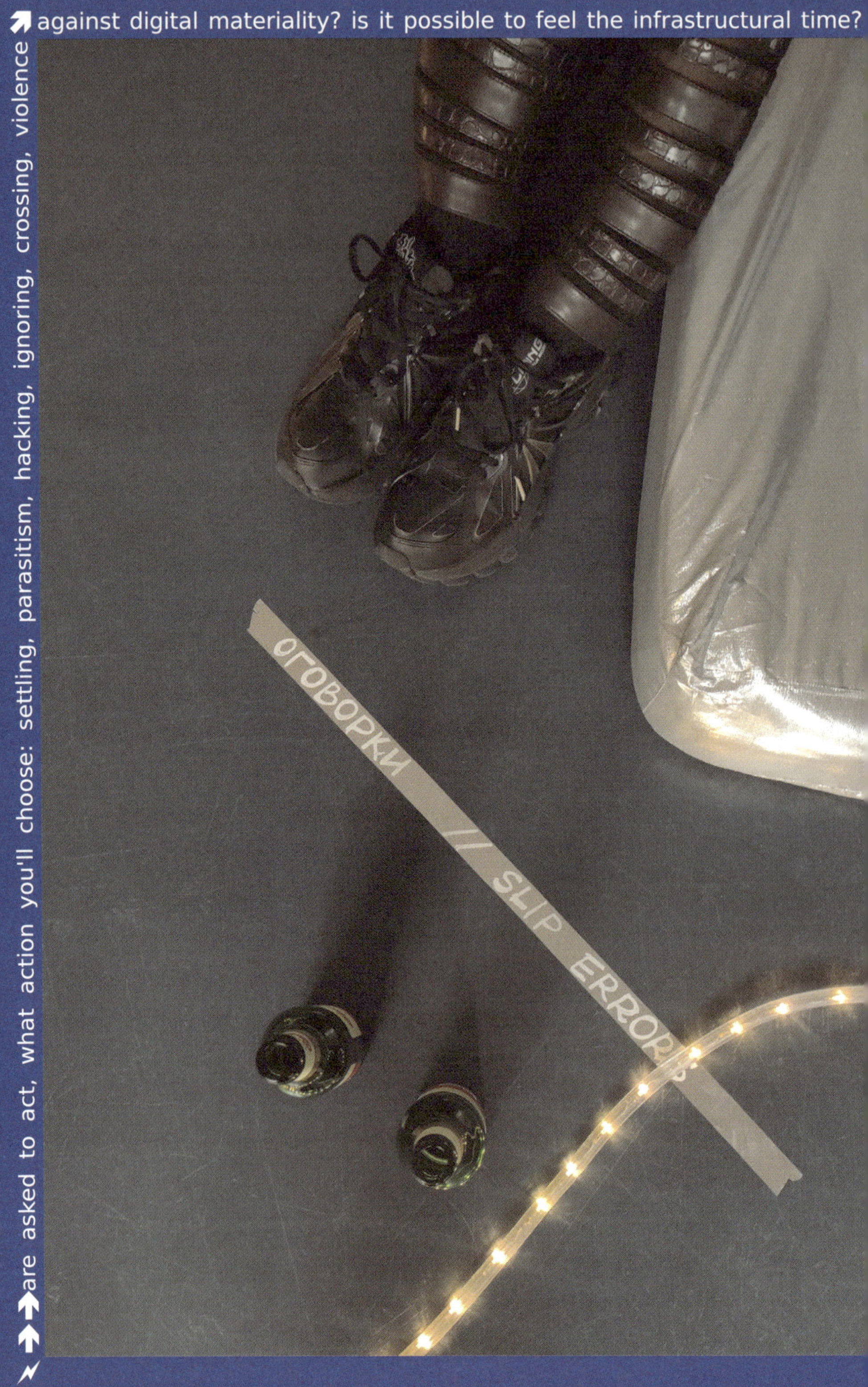

are asked to act, what action you'll choose: settling, parasitism, hacking, ignoring, crossing, violence against digital materiality? is it possible to feel the infrastructural time?

how to steal the diamond of knowledge? too close to reality? at what point do virtual maps become real? your question here

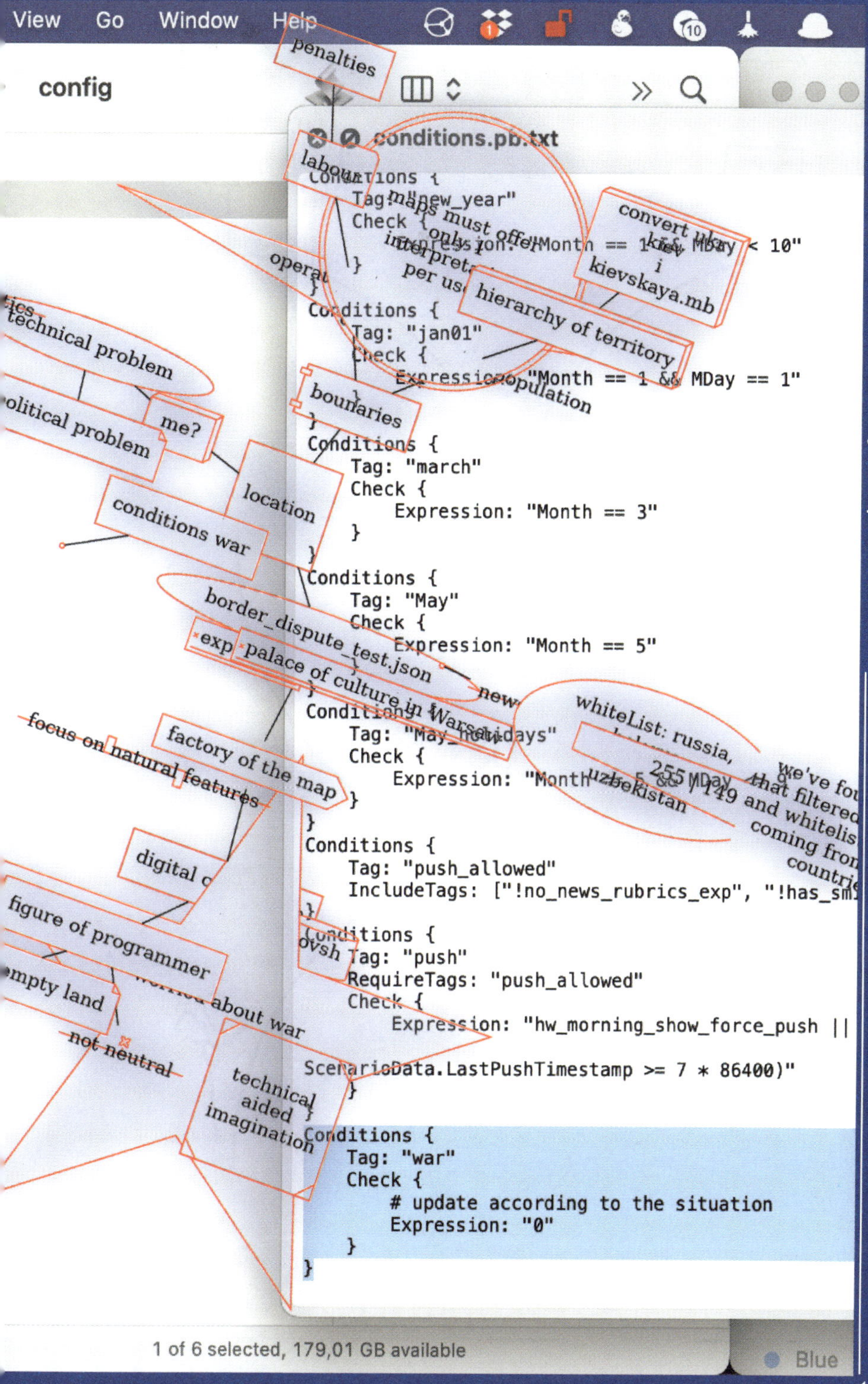

View Go Window Help

config

conditions.pb.txt

```
Conditions {
    Tag: "new_year"
    Check {
        Expression: "Month == 1 && MDay < 10"
    }
}
Conditions {
    Tag: "jan01"
    Check {
        Expression: "Month == 1 && MDay == 1"
    }
}
Conditions {
    Tag: "march"
    Check {
        Expression: "Month == 3"
    }
}
Conditions {
    Tag: "May"
    Check {
        Expression: "Month == 5"
    }
}
Conditions {
    Tag: "May_holidays"
    Check {
        Expression: "Month == 5 && MDay
    }
}
Conditions {
    Tag: "push_allowed"
    IncludeTags: ["!no_news_rubrics_exp", "!has_sm
}
Conditions {
    Tag: "push"
    RequireTags: "push_allowed"
    Check {
        Expression: "hw_morning_show_force_push ||

ScenarioData.LastPushTimestamp >= 7 * 86400)"
    }
}
Conditions {
    Tag: "war"
    Check {
        # update according to the situation
        Expression: "0"
    }
}
```

- penalties
- labour
- maps must offer only one interpretation per us
- operat
- convert ukr kiev i kievskaya.mb
- hierarchy of territory
- population
- boundaries
- technical problem
- me?
- political problem
- location
- conditions war
- border_dispute_test.json
- exp
- palace of culture in Warsaw
- new
- whiteList: russia, belarus, uzbekistan
- 255 / 149
- we've found that filtered and whitelis coming from countri
- focus on natural features
- factory of the map
- digital c
- figure of programmer
- worried about war
- empty land
- not neutral
- technical aided imagination
- ovsh

1 of 6 selected, 179,01 GB available

Blue

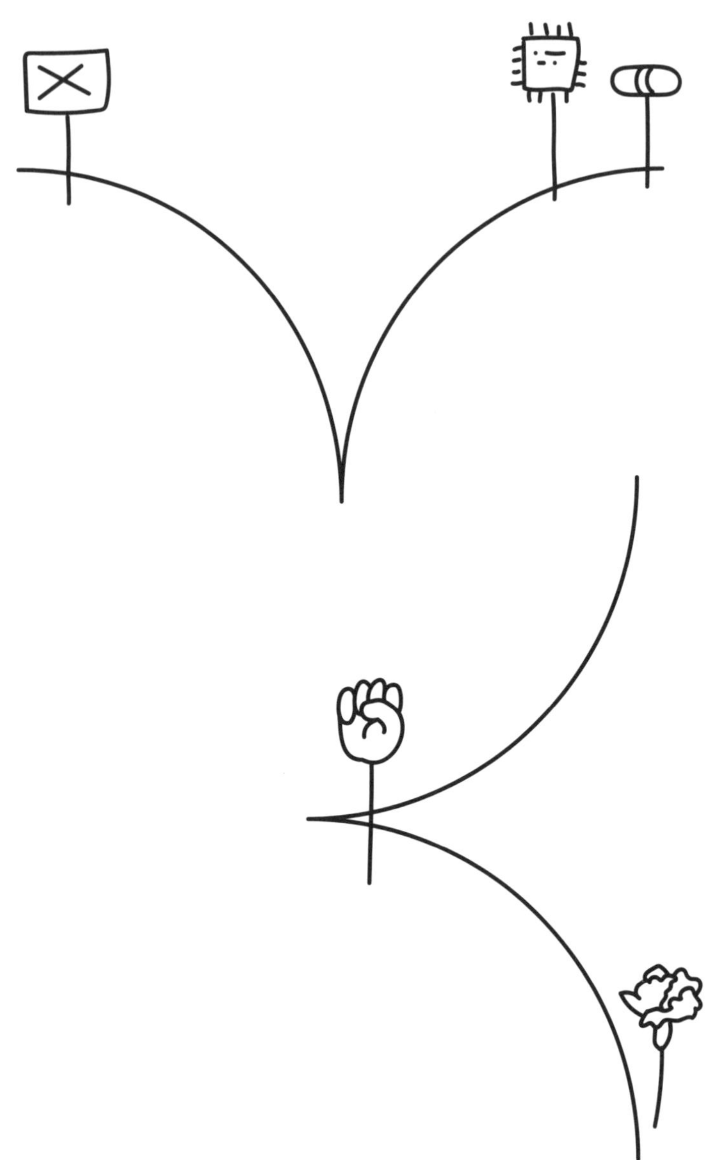

Unrest, Exhaustion, Care

A conversation
with
Marta Romankiv .... MR
Olia Sosnovskaya .... OS
and Maja Vusilović .... MV

Moderated by
Aleksei Borisionok .... AB

The idea of a conversation between Marta Romankiv, Olia Sosnovskaya, and Maja Vusilović emerged within the turbulent context of labor struggles, strikes and the unfolding imperialist war of Russia against Ukraine in recent years. Artist Marta Romankiv, researcher and artist Olia Sosnovskaya, and writer and union organizer Maja Vusilović delve into the intertwined themes of unrest, exhaustion, and care within the context of their diverse activist and artistic practices. Proposing various interpretations of post-socialism and acute forms of solidarity, the conversation focuses on the political organization of one of the most vulnerable groups in society, namely care workers, prompting critical reflections on (in)visibility, autonomy, labor unrest and unionization.

AB Thank you very much for joining the discussion. I would like to start our conversation with a question that helps us to think about the scale of our struggles. This is also a methodological question concerning the ways in which we can define our geographies and temporalities. In the Biennale Matter of Art, we as curators are also interested in the ways that the time that followed the forms of

state socialism informed our social bonds, ways of organizing and various other political horizons. Both Kateřina Kolářová and Tomasz Rakowski in their anthropological research, fragments of which are presented in this publication, navigate us through the ways in which we can understand post-socialism. So I would like to ask you to expound your visions regarding the geographies we are speaking about today, and explain how they make sense to you. Is the notion of post-socialism of any value, or do you rather find it damaging and corrupted?

OS Indeed, there have been a lot of critiques of this notion. It was summarized pretty well in the article "Goodbye, Postsocialism!" (2019) by Martin Müller.[1] First of all, this notion homogenizes very diverse and complex experiences, and in addition it obscures the intra-imperial relations in the region. Also, this discourse is often Moscow-centric and only refers to the experience of the Soviet Union, which is equated with Russia. Besides that, Russia itself hijacks many of the legacies of (post-)socialism and uses them in order to justify its imperial invasions. The temporality of post-socialism is often seen as always referring to the past, in which the future never arrives—the prefix "post" is about constant catching up. It also stifles political imagination: after the end of post-socialism, the only alternative is capitalism. And what's been interesting for me is the issue of how to think about post-socialism in relation to postcolonialism and decolonial movements. And this is also a very uneasy relationship. The post-socialist region has been rendered irrelevant by the West, but also by the global South, and has been mostly excluded from decolonial or postcolonial discourses.

I am interested in the ideas expressed by Neda Atanasoski and Kalindi Vora,[2] who claim that socialism is a global condition. Russia's war in Ukraine also is very important in exerting further pressure for the need to rethink post-socialism. But as I've said, for me, the writings of Neda Atanasoski and Kalindi Vora have been very inspiring because they actually believe that post-socialism could still be a useful analytical and conceptual tool to challenge the idea of state socialism as the only form of socialism. And they also want to challenge the idea that postcolonialism is only valid for the countries of the Global South, whereas post-socialism is only relevant to Central Asia, Eastern Europe and former Soviet states, which leads to a situation in which these geographies become totally separated.

MR Thank you, Olia. I would like to pick up on the issue of the post-socialist era you've referred to. As a Ukrainian, I think a lot changed after 2014, and finally after Russia's full-scale invasion of Ukraine in 2022. Many people felt an urge to separate from the oppressor, from Russia. I think that first of all, within this context, defining these various countries under a single common denominator is highly problematic, as it blurs the responsibility for the colonial past of Russia, but also of the Soviet Union. It makes accountability for acts of oppression and crimes unclear. Moreover, it creates a uniform gray mass from the diverse cultures and histories of different regions that have their own history and continuity. So therefore I find this notion rather problematic.

Returning to the question—my practice is derived from the specific context. I live and work mostly in Poland, though I come from Lviv, Ukraine. Therefore I am particularly interested in another type of

1
Martin Müller, "Goodbye, Postsocialism!" *Europe-Asia Studies* 71, no. 4 (2019): 533–550, https://doi.org/10.1080/09668136.2019.1578337.

2
Lesia Pagulich and Tatsiana Shchurko, "(Re)thinking Postsocialism: Interview with Neda Atanasoski and Kalindi Vora," *Feminist Critique*, no. 3 (2020): 91–111.

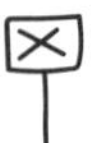

geography, namely the border of the European Union. In some of my projects the essential question is this—what is Europe and where is its border? Before and especially now, the question of East-Central Europe is very important, as it deals with politics of inclusion and exclusion, labor migration, displacement and so on. Also I remember when I was nineteen, when Euromaidan started, the question of belonging to the European political community was very important for all the people around me. And I have a feeling that back then and now in the Ukrainian discourse, the question of belonging to Europe often arises, in both cultural and political contexts. This affiliation is becoming a fact, not a question, but I still notice how often people in Ukraine use the word "Europe" in the sense of meaning something that is outside. In these moments I ask myself what does "Europe" mean? It is with this question that my video performance *I dreamed about Europe* started almost in an autobiographical way.

I grew up near the Western border of Ukraine, seventy kilometers from the Polish–Ukrainian border—but for me Europe was much further away, something that belonged to the West. And it was something of a different order, something from the future. During the preparation of the video performance I composed a text of excerpts from Ukrainian articles written after 2012 that relate to the idea of Europe, as well as to the understanding of Europeanness. During the video performance, I read the text. This work was also the beginning for the conception of the next project under the title *Euroworkshop*, where I invited migrants with different backgrounds who are living in Poland but who don't have EU citizenship. I asked them what Europe meant to them and what Europe should look like. What is the Europe of their dreams actually like? We recorded video statements from these people, which became part of the installation work. And here we can also move on to the second very important topic for me—the topic of citizenship, its limitations and exclusivity.

Here we can see a paradox that people are paying taxes, working and living in a country, but they don't have access to political rights in their place of residence. I see a lot of connections with the situation of women a little over a hundred years ago. Women fought for their political rights, winning the right to vote. Now, in most countries, migrants are a group excluded from politics, for example in terms of voting rights. During the course of my PhD research I found a postcard created by Suffrage Atelier that says—"no taxation without representation." In my opinion it perfectly connects feminist struggles with the struggles of migrants. I think that what affects us all should be approved by everyone. Therefore, in my artistic and activist practice I pay attention to issues of political rights and these questions of inclusion of the most vulnerable and invisible groups—for example care workers.

MV My primary focus is not migration itself, but it seems like migration always comes through in my work. Ten years after moving to the Czech Republic from Croatia, the topic of migration comes to the surface no matter what I write about or what my practice looks like. Thinking about post-socialism is very interesting for me, as I'm a person who's moved from one post-socialist country to another. We, as oppressed people, which I consider myself to be, were never really allowed to understand post-socialism. We were never really allowed to comprehend and process it. In the Czech Republic, I feel myself trapped between a rock and a hard place—aspiration to the West and self-colonization, on the one hand, and leaving our Eastern European identity in the shadows on the other. In Croatia, this manifests itself in a form of destructive tourism, which Croatia is totally overwhelmed by. In that sense, self-colonization is an important topic for me. We always look up to the West instead of building alliances between our peers—namely other post-socialist countries. We, as union organizers, look up to the West too much instead of building strategic partnerships between the countries that surround us and that share a rich experience from the past with us. I think the true strength lies in that.

We don't have a massive feminist and/or union movement in the Czech Republic yet, but we do take a lot of inspiration, for example, from the Polish union movement. The Polish feminist and union movement is very strong, especially if we talk about the care sector, where there are large numbers of migrant workers. This sector is built on the exploitation of informal working contracts or no contracts at all, which makes union organizing so much more complicated. Still, the people who are deeply invested in organizing in this sector are so good at what they do. They manage to find opportunities and ways to negotiate—even in situations where you have no one to negotiate with because you work without a contract (you just come to the family's house and work for them). So far I've had an opportunity to collaborate with union movements from Poland, Croatia and Hungary. But honestly it is my dream to be a part of a mass feminist union movement in Central/Eastern Europe. This is something that we should aspire to, because it could really work well for all of us.

Every time I went to Poland with my union, I came back so motivated and so fascinated by their practices. Sharing our knowledge and lived experience leads to building solidarity—our experience of being exploited and oppressed is somehow not unique. When I was in Croatia this year, I had an opportunity to talk to care workers there. The problems workers face there are the same as those my comrades face here in the Czech Republic. Sometimes they even work for the same corporations. Their bosses are the same. So why not inspire each other? When I met the workers in Croatia, we spoke about what they considered to be unimaginable at the given moment—bargaining for a collective agreement. I then told them this had already been done in the Czech Republic or in Poland. Our conversation shifted at that moment.

AB Can you please speak about the contexts of your struggles in more detail, so it can help us to navigate through different scales? Olia, you have just published an article on feminist politics and the poetics of disruption during the social uprising in Belarus, where different forms of labor unrest were very important.

OS Regarding the notion of a feminist strike, my idea wasn't to debate whether the protests in 2020 were feminist or not. Women were extremely active in the uprising—there was also significant female representation among the presidential candidates. However, it's important to acknowledge that despite the active participation of women, it's not always accurate to categorize those protests as explicitly feminist. In my analysis, I suggested approaching the very dynamics of the protests through a feminist lens, beyond the spectacular, heroic acts of disruption that revolutions are mostly associated with. The protest movement involved not only overt displays of dissent but also the establishment of new relationships and networks of care. Addressing political exhaustion is also essential within this framework. I focused particularly on the wave of strikes during the uprising, which, despite taking unconventional forms, marked a most significant wave of labor unrest in the post-socialist context. These forms encompassed various activities such as participating in

demonstrations or redirecting efforts towards activist work or other forms of engagement. The Ukrainian scholar Volodymyr Artiukh published an excellent study on this issue.[3]

Moreover, I examined the transformation of mass protest marches into regular neighborhood gatherings, highlighting the importance of sustaining collective action beyond public demonstrations. These gatherings, sometimes more celebratory than openly political, emerged as responses to state repression and served as platforms for building mutual support networks, underscoring the need to adapt and innovate forms of prefigurative resistance. Anarchist groups played a significant role in this movement. It also has informed my thinking about failure and burnout, not in solely negative terms but as a certain continuity and mundanity of political agency, something that perhaps can turn into strategy. Those practices resonate with other uprisings, as happened for example during the Arab Spring, when the daily practices of people were part of the resistance, but were not registered as resistance by the state.

The notion of prefigurative politics is crucial in order to emphasize the importance of daily practices and solidarity networks in pursuing revolutionary change, even if immediate transformation isn't imminent. We have observed the emergence of various small initiatives aimed at supporting political prisoners and countering state propaganda, which persisted even during the full-scale Russian invasion of Ukraine. When Russian troops entered Belarus under the guise of military training and attacked Ukraine, civil society was already devastated. The number of political prisoners had surged to around

3
Volodymyr Artiukh, "The Anatomy of Impatience: Exploring Factors behind 2020 Labour Unrest in Belarus," *Slavic Review* 80, no. 1 (Spring 2021): 52–60, https://doi.org/10.1017/slr.2021.26.

fifteen hundred, with many individuals forced to flee the country. Despite the heightened risks, people continued to protest. The invasion of Ukraine by Russian forces further complicated the landscape of resistance in Belarus. Despite the increased risks, existing networks of support and organization adapted to address new challenges, such as supporting refugees, countering state propaganda and directly sabotaging the military infrastructure. This period has underscored the need for both continuity and adaptability in resistance efforts, particularly in the face of escalating violence. Nevertheless, the exigencies of war have challenged the notion of gradual, subtle support gestures, demanding a more urgent and militant response, including military action. This dichotomy has led to a split within various feminist groups, with some advocating peaceful anti-war resistance, while others, including many Ukrainian feminists, emphasize the necessity of militant self-defense.

AB Maja and Marta, unlike the spontaneous character of labor unrest in Belarus within the context of the state instrumentalization of unions and the destruction of independent unions, you are working on long-term union organizing projects in the Czech Republic and Poland. Can you share your experience of organizing care with us? What relations of visibility/invisibility are implied there?

MV The most transformative practice I've learned to exercise in my union is actually listening. When we work with the oppressed, when we connect as oppressed to other oppressed, we need to place a big emphasis on sharing our experience because no one else will give a damn about us. No one wants to hear our stories, of how hard it is to work in care and how underpaid we are. We are not even allowed to express what we are going through. If we

don't have the opportunity to articulate our experiences, it will be challenging to contextualize our struggles. This is what we as union organizers want to change. That's why, during one-to-one conversations with workers, I always begin by asking, "How are you doing?" It may seem a simple and banal question, but this question is actually surprisingly useful. In my experience, no one asks the workers this question, no one wants to know what their working day looks like or how they are changing the diapers of their clients in care homes for the elderly, for example. By acknowledging and validating their anger and frustration that comes out of the unjust working conditions they work under, we can establish trust and develop strategies for how to mobilize and unite workers within our movement.

How does feminism intersect with our union-organizing efforts? I believe this intersection lies in maintaining a non-hierarchical, or at least less top-down structure within the union, which may seem contradictory to some. A top-down union is, at least in my opinion, a paradox. It might aim to bring more people together, but as you've likely observed in your own countries, unions often become part of the establishment. Our struggle can begin within the union, but then its impact must extend far beyond, influencing how we conceive of society as a whole. Union work might start with negotiating for better pay, but the fight never ends. The negotiations never end.

There's a distinction between the struggling union work and what's often termed a service union. You might be familiar with the concept of a service union, where you pay your dues monthly and then receive benefits like legal protection or even a gift at the end of the year. These unions provide services, but they lack the radical, collective approach of struggling unions.

In contrast, struggling unions engage members in every aspect of the struggle. While strikes are a powerful form of protest, I believe we shouldn't view them as a last resort but rather as a right that we should exercise more frequently. However, the real challenge lies in the day-to-day work: the weekly meetings, the note-taking, the coordination. This is the real heavy lifting. We've seen several large mobilizations fizzle out due to a lack of sustained follow-up and organization. And this is the reason why we should aim at establishing struggling unions that engage their members in all aspects of the union work and take collective action. This is what brings the workers agency. A strong union means a visible union. Nothing is achieved as a secret union. But being visible is sometimes a real privilege, because not everyone can be visible, especially in a union. Being visible as a union member sometimes means that you know you will not be at the workplace tomorrow. But then we as more privileged union members should do the work and represent our comrades publicly, or until our union gets stronger.

Lastly, the feminist part of organizing in care is all about seizing the means of social reproduction. How are we to explain this? If your work is looking after people in a home for the elderly by providing them with care, then the results of your labor are often used for a further accumulation of the capital that corporations own. We should take the means of our labor back and use them to build a new society, not help corporations get richer every day.

MR We see that migrants often are a very stigmatized group. In many cases, they are considered victims. This takes possible agency from them. I'm putting a lot of effort into reversing this. Maja just said that to be visible is a privilege. And this becomes clear in union work as well as in artistic practice. Actually, through art and activism it is possible to reverse this invisibility—visibility dichotomy.

The initiative *You Can Count On Me* began in 2021 during my residency in Warsaw. It was during this time that I encountered care workers and became acutely aware of the challenges they face. Many work under extremely difficult conditions: without contracts, often working 24/7 without respite, and frequently residing at their workplace due to the low wages that prevent them from affording separate accommodation. They don't have places for rest and leisure time. This situation is particularly common among migrant workers, who come seeking better opportunities but find themselves trapped in exploitative conditions.

I observed these conditions and realized there was no union or organization addressing the needs of domestic and care workers in Poland. Due to the lack of contracts, we have little data on the number of people employed in this sector, which operates largely in the shadows. There was a clear absence of support structures for these workers. After numerous conversations with individuals, primarily from Ukraine, I recognized the need for a space where they could come together, share experiences, and feel heard.

They often struggle with the language barrier, making it difficult to participate in cultural events. Many have told me that they spend their free time aimlessly wandering around shopping malls because they lack social connections and opportunities to engage in activities. Recognizing this, I felt compelled to create a space for them to meet. I saw the importance of regular gatherings. It was also crucial that we had a small house in Warsaw with a garden where they could grow plants and vegetables. I also began inviting people from trade unions and other organizations that support migrants' rights advocacy groups to our meetings. After about four months, we collectively decided to establish a trade union for domestic workers in Poland. This

Domestic Workers Committee (Komisja Pracownic i Pracowników Domowych), operating up to now under the umbrella of the larger union Workers' Initiative (Inicjatywa Pracownicza), was officially established two and a half years ago. While I initiated this space as an artist, I'm uncertain whether to categorize it as an artistic or activist endeavor. I'm still helping them in various ways – organizing events, translating, managing their social media and so on. My role in this initiative has always been to empower them to speak for themselves. I'm thrilled to see members of the trade union stepping up to participate in interviews, advocate for themselves and regain their own agency.

The notion of care is very much connected to relations of visibility and invisibility. It's about visibility, or rather, invisibility – the frequently overlooked work that underpins the cultural sector and economy. We rarely acknowledge the domestic labor that supports every poet, artist, or other historical figure. Someone did most of their domestic work for them. And we probably wouldn't have so many important figures, whose monuments are now in public spaces, if they'd had to manage all their domestic tasks themselves. It's essential to remember the individuals behind these prominent names. For example, in 2022, during a May 1st demonstration near the Adam Mickiewicz monument in Kraków, members of the Domestic Workers Committee carried a painting with the slogan: "Where is the monument of the housemaid?" As part of this action, we wanted to raise the issue of who is visible and who needs more visibility in our public space.

MV Thank you, Marta, for your insights. Building on what you've said, I think that every conversation about care should be focused on addressing invisibility. Whether it's formal or informal, whether it's performed in the workplace or at home–care

is always equally exploited. We say that care work is invisible, but care can also be hypervisible, and therefore invisible in its hypervisibility because it's everywhere around us. Everything in the world revolves around care, but somehow care work means little when it comes to the material aspect of it, when care is not even recognized as a work. I think that our task as organizers, as feminists, as revolutionaries is to build on that—to take back the stereotypes and build on them as women, as gender non-conforming people and queers.

Nowadays there is a new language we can use in order to speak about care work and call these phenomena by their right name. The theory of social reproduction is finally gaining more popularity, not only in the feminist movement. For example, in her a new book, Alva Gotby[4] teaches us that we are forced to learn how to care and how to be good at it. So what she says is that no one is born a good carer, we all get good at it by practicing it very often. We should use those abilities that we were forced to learn in order to liberate ourselves from oppression and subjection to exploitation. We should take these tools back and use them for our revolution. It is possible that our work might not be recognized by society, but we can be actors in changing this reality that does not recognize our work. Liberal feminism tells us that washing dishes is the problem, and that we should find someone who'll wash our dishes for us. Well, I think the problem is not in doing the dishes but in the ideology that surrounds it. What we can get rid of is this ideology that causes care to be undervalued and outsourced via capitalist structures to the others who are doing this work—to migrants, and to people who are stripped of their own agency and political subjectivity.

4
Alva Gotby, *They Call It Love: The Politics of Emotional Life* (London: Verso, 2023).

And again to the question of visibility and invisibility. Privileged people should be visible, and they should work to make our union so strong that even the vulnerable people with short-term contracts can also be visible. We, as organizers, should be invisible. It is our workers whom we should make visible. We should pass on the tools. Of course, in many cases it doesn't work like that. I sometimes feel that I'm the one who gets more from the workers than they get from me. This is why I think that organizing is like a pedagogy of the oppressed, where you never know who's the teacher and who's the student. Radical gestures such as strikes are good, but what we are doing every day is equally important, because meetings are often scarier and more difficult than strikes.

AB Here I would like to invite you to think about solidarities, their possibilities in current contexts, their controversies. What kind of role are care and social reproduction playing in solidarity networks?

OS I must emphasize that the official unions in Belarus are heavily influenced by the state and often serve as vehicles for state propaganda. While there are independent unions, they weren't widely embraced until the wave of strikes in 2020, which prompted the creation of new unions as people left the official ones. I was actually thinking about vulnerability, care and solidarity in terms of political agency. During the protests in 2020 there was a huge wave of solidarity, which was also very unexpected and unprecedented. In terms of striking, I think the main problem is that not everyone can afford to strike when they could be fired so easily. So during the 2020 strikes in Belarus, people were sharing their incomes and donating massively to funds for those who were dismissed. Another important thing was that apart from general protest marches, there were regular marches of people with disabilities,

marches of the retired and marches of queer people and women. So those groups who are normally completely invisible within the public space and deprived of political agency were at the forefront of the struggle, while manifesting their vulnerability.

Speaking about solidarity, it's essential to address the refugee crisis on the border of Belarus, Poland, and Lithuania, which has been ongoing since 2021. It is a vivid example of how solidarity also fails to emerge just from the experience of vulnerability alone. Despite many Belarusian citizens themselves being forced to flee the dictatorial regime, experiencing state violence and repression, many showed little solidarity or even empathy toward refugees from Afghanistan, Iraq, Palestine and other countries in the Middle East and North Africa, who have been experiencing violent push-backs and extreme conditions stuck in the forest, and many of whom have died as a result. The Belarusian state instrumentalized their vulnerability to threaten the European Union. And thus, unfortunately, some protesters and independent media associated the refugees with the Belarusian regime, fomenting xenophobia and hindering possible solidarity, despite the fact that they shared some similar experiences. This situation prompts critical questions about navigating different forms of imperialism, such as Western and Russian, and acknowledging multiple regimes of oppression and vulnerability without oversimplifying solidarity based solely on shared experiences of oppression. We should recognize and address the complexities of privilege, hierarchies, and inequalities when striving for genuine solidarity. In Eastern Europe people are both underprivileged and embedded in different regimes of oppression, such as whiteness. The Belarusian queer feminist scholar Tatsiana Shchurko has a great text on why solidarity between Black Lives Matter and Belarusian protests in 2020 didn't happen.[5]

MR I can briefly add two points building on what Olia's just said. We know a lot about how hard it is to build anti-imperialist solidarity in the context of war. Ukrainians saw a lack of solidarity from Western leftists in 2022 because their filters didn't fit the new situation and they failed to recognize the multiple forms of imperialism that are not only connected with US imperialism. I also want to remind us of the slogan, which was very popular last year—"pacifism is a privilege." People who haven't experienced the shelling of their family house would not probably understand people with this experience. So solidarity probably couldn't work in every case, but I hope it will.

Today, real opposition to Russian imperialism can only be achieved by military force, for example by the Ukrainian army. But in the perspective of long-term strategies that can change imperialist thinking in general, I personally believe in unions and labor organizations. Being a worker is often a common experience for many people from different parts of the world. It can also be helpful in building grassroots and transnational structures, as well as self-organization on an equal basis. This activation of society and the belief that we, as residents of specific areas, can have an impact on things that affect us, can probably also influence the deconstruction of imperialist thinking, which is largely based on subordination.

MV I'd really like to respond to what you said, Marta, about pacifism being a privilege. I am very triggered by the Westsplaining that is directed at us every time there is a war going on in our region.

5
Tatsiana Shchurko, "From Belarus to Black Lives Matter: Rethinking protests in Belarus through a transnational feminist perspective," *Intersections: East European Journal of Society and Politics* 8, no. 4 (January 2023): 25–41, https://doi.org/10.17356/ieejsp.v8i4.1007.

I was born in the ’90s, just before the war started in Croatia. The experience of war is a traumatic event that affected me and my whole family. This is why I’m really worried about the selective solidarity and false moralism on the part of the West.

For me solidarity is in the union movement, it’s as vital as negotiation. There is no negotiation without solidarity. And as you said, there are always different ways in which we can engage with the movement, even if we’re not visible. We can speak of solidarity also in the terms of mutual help—for me it’s also the basics of unionizing.

People are meant to solidarize with other people, it’s just that capitalism forces us to cultivate competition. We can either solidarize with other people or we can compete and shape ourselves as neoliberal individuals. And as time goes by, I hope that we as a movement can also express solidarity, not only with other union movements but with other movements as well—for example the anti-colonial and liberation movement in Palestine. I wish more unions would express their solidarity with the people of Palestine.

OS Right, coming back to the issue of invisibility and care, violence against people in Gaza is clearly visible, but as you said—it becomes invisible in its hypervisibility.

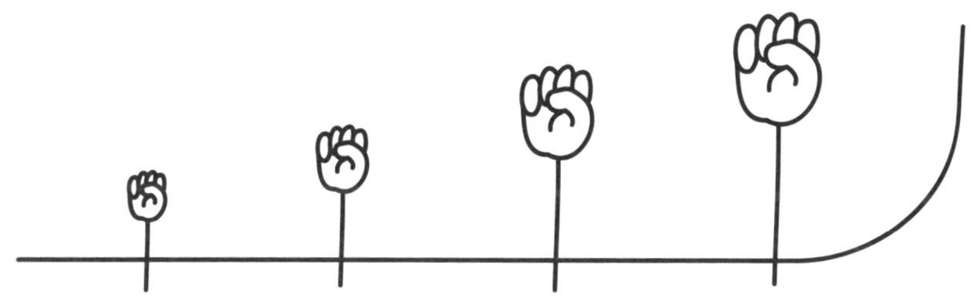

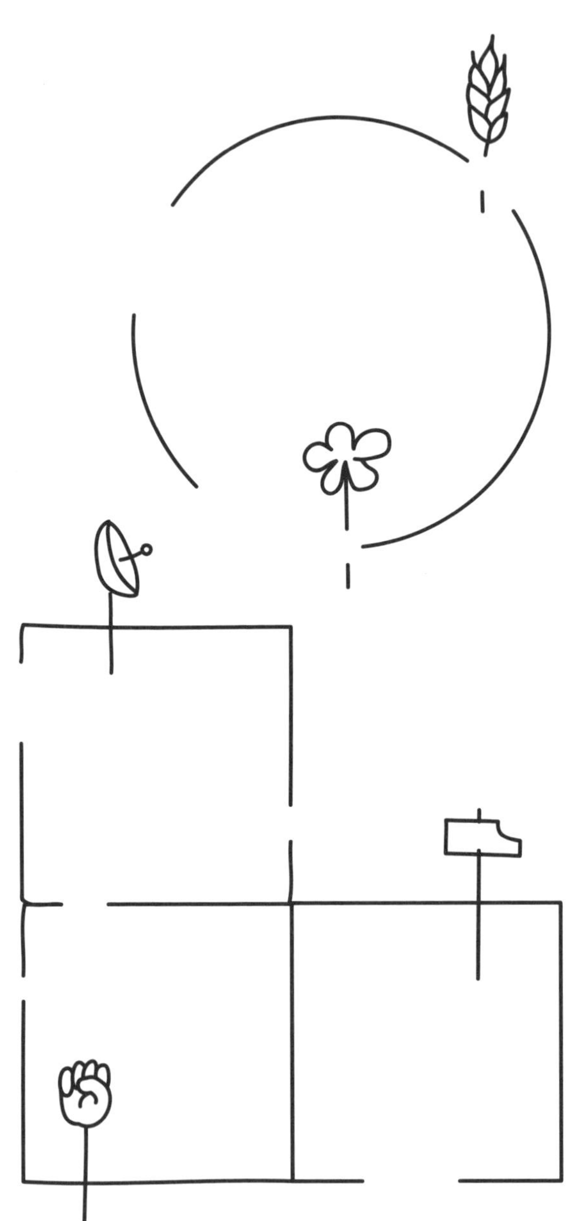

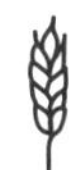

Rural People: Other Histories, Alternative Materialities, and a Turn to Freedom

Tomasz Rakowski

Being of rural descent, having a peasant background, relocating from the countryside to urban areas, the men sporting a cotton wool-padded jacket and beret, the women wearing a headscarf amidst seemingly isolated landscapes with potato, rapeseed, and maize fields in the background—all these visual representations have, for decades, been the soft underbelly of the ongoing discourse surrounding contemporary social relations within the modernizing region of Central and Eastern Europe. These dynamics pertain not only to interpersonal relationships and those between people and animals but also to individuals' inner conflicts. They encompass narratives, emotions, judgements, essays, and even scholarly papers, whose continuity may appear overwhelming. I believe that our attitude toward the countryside and rural people reflects the entirety of contemporary social interactions and social existence.

How can we understand the experiences of rural people in Central and Eastern Europe?

The discussion about the rural genealogies of Central European societies is tied to their rural peripherality and, to a large extent, to a distinctly different form of rural life compared to Western countries. Historically, in these countries farming has been more extensive, less efficient, and less modernized than in Western Europe. As a result, they have a more agricultural character, cultivating significantly larger areas of land than their Western counterparts. In the post-war socialist countries, dependent on the Soviet Union, agricultural farms were transformed into state enterprises and cooperatives, which, on consolidated and collectivized lands, led to the development of new rural working environments. At the same time, various ways of combining work in state enterprises with individual farming emerged, as people raised animals for personal use and cultivated vegetable gardens on their household farms.

Only in Poland did individual farms largely remain intact; people effectively resisted the subsequent waves of forced collectivization until the 1960s, when the entire collectivization project was eventually abandoned. But overall, agriculture and work on rural farms in Central and Eastern Europe was more challenging and laborious, with cultivation being less intensive, less mechanized, and less efficient than in Western Europe. As time went on, this labor was often combined with factory work, people would tend to the land only after finishing their factory shifts. Finally, during the 1970s, in many cases agricultural villages underwent a noticeable and even enthusiastic modernization, which was later put on hold. When the 1990s arrived and a democratic era dawned in East Central Europe, these rural areas became particularly vulnerable to changes, experiencing a decline in agricultural production. Existing forms of work in state cooperatives were dismantled, leaving people without a livelihood or in imploding conditions, especially on small farms, which proved unprofitable in post-transitional Poland. It was in these regions that the most significant challenges emerged: unemployment and a lack of training for new non-agricultural, office-based, knowledge-reliant jobs.

The continuity of stereotypes

These rural people were frequently accused of impeding change, of being a burden on emerging societies, representing a form of vestige and an uninteresting facet of social life. In Poland, these debates have been intense and ongoing since the 1990s, evolving into a recurring narrative that attributes the rural origins of many Poles to an undeveloped civic culture, reluctance to engage in public and social activities, and a strong inclination towards accumulation, possession, and consumption.

I find it hard to accept this belief around me in Poland that prevails among journalists, columnists, and even social researchers. Those writing about the rural origins of the modern middle class, interpreting the countryside and rurality, and attempting to understand "Polish ruralness" touch upon the essential aspects of a quiet social history in Central and Eastern Europe. By "quiet," I mean that it unfolds slowly, beneath the surface, yet carries profound consequences. It is the social history of a country where rural overpopulation was at its highest, and the rural landscape was not as modern or efficient as, for instance, in socialist Czechoslovakia. Nor was it as centralized and collectivized as in other countries. In the post-war era, Polish society initially thrived in rural areas. It was the children of this rural population who, right after the war, headed in large numbers to agricultural and technical schools, then on to occupations in heavy and light industries, as well as jobs in hospitals, schools, offices, and the police force. The demand for labor in the new socialist post-war state—much like in other "people's democracies"—appeared almost limitless for the first time in history. Some worked in rural areas, some both here and there, commuting between the countryside and the city, while others migrated, settling permanently in urban centers.

The interpretations of these experiences, shaped by journalists and academics—often sociologists—largely portrayed rural people as a social, political, and technical residue, a persistent burden formed over the course of decades of socialist transformation. However, in my view, these images seem to focus less on the actual social history and more on attempting to convey how present Polish society needs to change and what it should be like. It reflects a desire for action—sometimes even an activist one—the yearning of "public intellectuals" whose energy, hopes, and skills permeate social life. For them, depictions of rurality are projections of the action, thought, and understanding of this particular group. I do not mean to suggest that such thinking is disconnected from reality, as it does, to some extent, confirm the truth about the structure and trajectory of rural transformations. Nevertheless, it remains a Pandora's box.

Let us go back to the origins of these stereotypes and their socio-cultural context. If we closely examine evaluations of social life, it becomes evident that rurality and peasantry are synonymous with something one should quickly disentangle from. This perception casts a shadow of trauma over the lives of contemporary Poles, a theme explored in recent engaged works by academics and journalists (such as Pobłocki's *Chamstwo* [The Rabble], Kuciel-Frydryszak's *Chłopki* [Peasant Women] and Rauszer's *Bękarty pańszczyzny* [Bastards of Serfdom]). But in journalistic discussions, a recurring theme suggests that rurality encapsulates fundamental deficiencies that prevail in our society. These deficiencies are familial loyalty, attachment to material possessions, greed, opportunism, the struggle for survival, tendencies towards populism, and an aversion, along with a demanding stance, towards the powerful and wealthy–formerly the manor, today represented by the institutions of the European Union and the state. A tone of judgment and civilizational superiority can be detected in this journalism, highlighting the perceived backwardness and unpreparedness of rural people to assume public, intellectual roles or belong to the bourgeois class. Some authors seem to suggest that the society of tomorrow will only be possible in Poland if it is void of political practices stemming from informal and largely uncontrolled village agreements and self-organized bodies like country housewives' associations or volunteer fire brigades.

I find such a perspective on society and its ongoing processes troubling, as it is largely dismissive of a form of understanding that is embedded in the ethnographic experience that I hold so dear. It presupposes that there is a predefined, legitimate interpretation of social history and a designated group of actors who are authorized to define it.

Unraveling rural peasant genealogies, in this line of thinking, is equated with explaining a perceived "flaw" ingrained in the newly emerging society. The village serves as a framework for us to ponder what constitutes a "rightful" social life, as well as the "appropriate" assimilation of experiences and skills—almost a form of re-education. Often, the lives of the residents, their social, political, and artistic endeavors, remain on the sidelines, overlooked. Hence, it is worth examining this phenomenon from a more ethnographic angle and trying to shift this perspective.

Different histories, different people: village and ethnography

Gaining an understanding of rural experiences immediately calls for what could be termed decolonization. What does this mean? I am inclined to believe that the colonization process we are witnessing in Eastern Europe, especially in Polish society, is of particular consequence. It is the emergence of a social history written predominantly from the perspective of a single social group—the intelligentsia, sometimes former dissidents, participants in the "culture of dissent"—envisioning a desired future and process of societal modernization. Societal transformations are thus interpreted from their perspective. Strategies of rebellion and resistance against the socialist state, social movements, and good civic practices all emerge with the greatest historical impact not in the rural world but in cities, among the educated, aware, and public intellectuals.

Yet rural areas possess their own distinct history. Although largely disregarded by modernizers and opinion-makers, they have their own account of a "self-organizing" and "free" society. This includes the era of socialist Poland, perceived by contemporary rural residents as a time of remarkable journeys to urban schools and dormitories, years of vocational training and labor—often remembered with as much fascination and fondness as present-day anecdotes of students on Erasmus exchanges to European universities. It is a memory of how monotonous life in an impoverished village was suddenly transformed into a journey.

It is also about remembering how, in the 1970s, the village prospered, experiencing its "golden age"—at least, that is how it is preserved in the rural collective memory and described in research on rural production cooperatives in Hungary, among others by Chris Hann.

In Poland, what many would consider a typical socialist farce, the "social deed"—based on the Soviet-style idea of the "subbotnik" (volunteer work for the community)—is viewed quite differently in the accounts I have gathered from rural areas. It is perceived as a source of pride: coming together to build a school, a health center, or a community center, working with enthusiasm, sometimes late into the night. As part of the "Millennium Schools" program in Poland, schools were built across the country to commemorate the millennium of the Polish state. The original plan envisioned a thousand schools, yet more than twice as many were eventually constructed. In rural areas, they were built through collective efforts. The engineers lived among the people, villagers shared meals with them, and the completion of the school was celebrated multiple times afterwards. In various conversations, enthusiasm is overflowing, accompanied by the recurring use of the word "deed." The building of this health center was organized by the Community Council in Ostałówek. "Well, everyone had to pitch in, you know... Our deed was to lay the foundations, bring in the sand, all that..." In the village of Piekary, there are records in the fire brigade chronicles about putting on a small theater show in the community center to support their work. Tickets were sold to raise the money to build a fire station and buy a motor pump.

With the arrival of the next decade, dominated by protests and the eventual emergence of the Solidarność [Solidarity] movement, forms of resistance against authority also began to take shape in the villages. When the school construction program ended, efforts turned towards building churches for Roman Catholic parishes, also driven by community initiatives. People gave up their weekends to volunteer transporting building materials, and in the 1980s thousands of churches were erected, which was described by architecture researchers in the publication *Day-VII Architecture* (Izabela

Cichońska, Karolina Popera, Kuba Snopek). Churches and chapels were also built in rural areas, in defiance of party directives. Interestingly, party members were also involved in their construction, even though these buildings usually served as hubs for the opposition movement. They were also built as a social deed; the authors of *Day-VII Architecture* even came across a plaque proudly declaring that the church had been constructed as such. It reveals the structures of spontaneous cooperation and rural self-organization, which eagerly embraced the propaganda directive of social deeds. These stories also depict rural gatherings and community councils, which can now be understood as narratives of resistance and self-governance, giving rise to social autonomy.

In addition to the necessity of rural decolonization mentioned previously, a reevaluation of social history can be conducted through ethnographic research, which involves delving deeper into the rural world. Regarding the attitude of rural residents towards material possessions, it seems highly characteristic of their culture to accumulate everything that might come in handy. Hence, the significance of "having things" may appear to urban dwellers as inordinate thriftiness, frugality, and greed while prioritizing material values.
Once again, this is only partly true, or rather, an impression formed by outside observers. In the villages I know in central Poland, "possession" is all about protecting, enclosing, and storing—in the past, people used dowry chests, trunks, locked sheds, and fenced compounds. Owning something in the countryside is associated with a completely different attitude towards belongings and respecting their value—it is about the need to be self-sufficient and the desire to secure one's livelihood (storing raw materials, reserves such as barrels of oil, leftover building materials for a rainy day). In this other, sometimes baffling habit of collecting things with the mindset of "everything will come in handy," there is clearly a skill in managing what might appear unnecessary—components of devices, waste, and old tools. Here, we discuss a remarkable ability to adapt technology to suit one's needs. In rural areas, especially in the Podhale region, during the era of the People's Republic of Poland, and even until today, people made

their own devices. Not only because new factory models were unavailable but also because homemade devices were simply superior—they are self-built and inexpensive, and sometimes parts can be replaced more easily. Using an engine from a Fiat 126p car in a homemade tractor is seen as a major asset. In the Mazovia region, people craft lawnmowers, welding machines, and homemade tractors, while the young even design their own cars. These gadgets are made from spare parts collected "just in case." Such grassroots stories of technical ingenuity are documented in the collections of the Radomskie Countryside Museum or in Łukasz Skąpski's artistic works, initially dedicated to the remarkable homemade tractors from the Podhale region in the catalog *Machines*. They include tales of welding inventive hybrids from agricultural machinery or homemade tractors. One of them even received an award from local party authorities—a voucher for a holiday to Bulgaria. But almost the next day, he traded it for a set of tractor tires.

A turn to freedom

I am committed to uncovering such stories and cultural skills, to bring them to light as often as possible. My research is conducted in Polish villages, but in a similar yet distinct manner, forms of self-organization and informal communal activities thrived in agricultural Eastern Europe. If these alternative versions of history and culture are not explored, we risk being left with the one-sided narratives I mentioned before—narratives that portray rural culture as mere "baggage" that hinders the emergence of a "proper" middle class and a "proper" civil society. Therefore, I see a crucial need to change our mindset regarding the rural, peasant genealogy of societies after the political transformation of the 1990s. This decolonization will not occur merely by reviving the value of rural culture, its quiet histories, or experiences of urban migration. To truly achieve this, we must acknowledge that perceiving members of any social group as entirely shaped by culture, possessing a fixed cultural mindset ("the rural mentality"), is highly problematic and dangerous. In that case, culture becomes a form of enslavement; it is "inescapable" and takes on the nature of a "flaw" that can be hidden but cannot be banished. This happens if we do not perceive people as individual actors who are capable of transcending their cultural forms of existence—of being "someone else." As highlighted in anthropology by Nigel Rapport, acknowledging an individual's ability to "transcend oneself" restores their ability to truly "be oneself," to evolve. He writes about the moment of transcending oneself ("being someone else") in the process of migration and life transformation. In works such as *Anyone: The Cosmopolitan Subject of Anthropology*, he explores a unique point of inward turn, within an identity, illustrating how this publicized capacity for being "someone else" leads to adaptability in the face of cultural rules and norms.

The situation is genuinely paradoxical—if it is at all possible to understand the cultural uniqueness of rural people and their "peasant genealogy," it can only be achieved by discovering this fundamental, unrestricted freedom—freedom from cultural constraints. If we view the peasant or rural way of life and the process of "building oneself" as an inert, "descending" cultural disposition that hinders the rise of the middle class with its negative qualities, then this enslaving knowledge is perpetuated, colonizing people's own experiences. The goal, therefore, is to create a space for communication—exchange, and even, dare I say, closeness—among different social spheres, entities with different histories and social backgrounds, all within the realm of fundamental freedom from cultural constraints. Decolonization should involve creating a space where this fundamental right of all of us to be "someone else" can materialize.

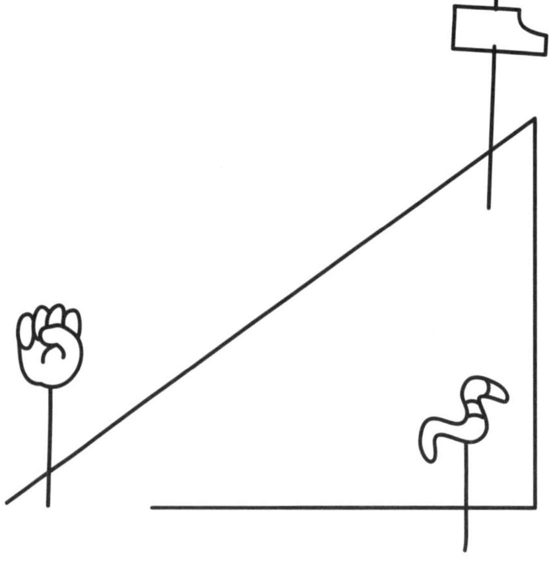

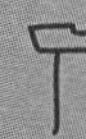

Galina Rymbu
2020

only our neighborhood had so many factories:
the Tire plant and the Tire Cord plant, then the Oxygen plant
(which no one ever saw—just gray boxes, neither smoke nor flame)
the Automation plant, the Brick and Asphalt factories, Power Plant
 No. 5,
the "Flight" factory and Cosmic Prospect, and this time repeated
as if in a memory—bathed in sunlight.
the ice cream factory and even in the cemetery near our building
a small factory that manufactured coffins.
and there were a lot of schools because people had a lot of kids
 and the boys all went into the army, and they
probably didn't even know why there was an army, and even more rarely
heard the word "armed forces,"
heard the word "history"...

this was our history, and now
it's become just a story solely about
how "the proletariat becomes the precariat"
and how the dark sun of prefab boggy blocks melts
in the light of new construction sites

it's about how to act
if they have a knife, and at any moment it
 could
and you have nothing but a desire to speak in another way
but with them
in their language

after all, soon there will be nothing but the straight line of history

and so, my father, as soon as he arrived in this city
he got a job at the "Flight" factory, which
produced parts
parts
parts
for space rockets
which the grandfather of my future husband
also constructed—

he used to go to The Armenia
but in the evenings, after a bit of vodka, they
played with the parts on the empty shop floor, like kids, and mom
taught in the polytechnic next to the factory
people went on from there to work at another factory
or—a little later—to kill, to love, to live

and the "Flight" factory closed down, and they leveled the ground and
put up new homes for people—
who are these people?

then he worked at the "Natural Siberian Rubber" factory
at a great height he repaired pipes filled with terrible compounds
ammonia
acid
benzoles
phenols
hell

at night they—he and his friends—would steal scrap metal and take it
through the "Oiler" neighborhood
to the receiving station (the road glistening after the rain) on a big truck,
with chansonnières on the radio—Tanya Bulanova, Irina Allegrova

but then
a pipe burst and the doorbell rang and they told us where our dad was
but basically that same morning he came back all bandaged up,
he'd run away, run home to us
his stomach was burned with acid and covered with pustulating scabs
and there were two drops on his face, too
which now form a peculiar scar on his temple and next to his eye

but then that factory closed down, too
or maybe they sold it, then sold it again (now to a Western company)
and my father lost his job

and he came home to us completely changed
and he forgot about fishing in the evenings behind the asphalt factory in our district
where he and I would throw maple whirlybirds in the autumn grove, as thick smoke curled across the sky
from the stacks of Power Plant No. 5

he also worked at the Tire plant which was close to where we lived
but he didn't work there for very long
in that place where black black tires rolled out for the cars of the future
for the people of the present, and as he thought—for our grandchildren, for your children
but I don't know what's happened to that rich, black factory now—
maybe that's gone, too?

but the people, where are the people?
they stayed, didn't they, didn't disappear along with the empty workshops
and their bones aren't resting under the tracks of bulldozers
they're working somewhere, aren't they, but it's
almost like they aren't there.
or are they?

who are we talking to?

also, when I was at school in the Cord settlement (that's where the Tire Cord plant was
and the Oxygen plant was somewhere nearby,
or at least there was a bus stop with that name, but I never saw the plant itself—
only gray cubes of the buildings without a single flame, without smoke);
even then I had the feeling that there would be some kind of conversation like this,
that sooner or later it would happen, it would begin,
and I didn't know who would be having it,
but I knew I wouldn't have anything to say.
how
will I possibly take part in it?
so it'll be like I'm somehow not here,
though I am still there,
but how can we avoid the eternal aggression of participation?
those were the days when the oil refinery still burned at the other end of town

and I've never seen a flame like that anywhere else
(how can I convey the intensity of that flame—should I say "fire,"
 "it's insane," "it's inside me"?)
even when the forests outside Moscow were burning and the animals
fled

<u>and the animals fled</u>

maybe that's why I can never understand—how? what does it mean—
 to write for workers?
what can it be to separate the wheat from the chaff for them
aren't these the grains of wheat, right here
aren't these the stones
isn't this experience
and if that's true, then what else, what more can I say to my father?
....
or maybe—those backward times,
when my father went off to do some other jobs at someone's dacha,
he also did carpentry, and he
cut off the fingers on his right hand with a power saw,
but they sewed them back on.
and he doesn't remember anything about it.
I'm four years old (when the line of history is straightest)
 we're sitting on the curb bandages mom dad and me
drinking peach juice
summer heat
next to the hospital bright flowerbeds with perennials
....
there will come a time when no one will remember this
....
and I
later learned how to read music
but never did manage to hear that music
to make others hear it
on the outskirts in a building (hum, hum) right next to the Russian,
 Muslim, and Jewish cemeteries,
the place where they take the people from the factories,
and then bring them flowers and chocolates.
and we, the kids, we run in the rain in May among the graves and we
 eat the chocolates.—

that's how the straight line of history runs out.
and later in the courtyard with the garages we summon up a witch,
and one girl even says she sold her soul to the devil for a bag of candy,
 some fish, and a new ceiling lamp.

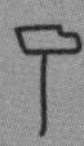

there isn't one single metaphor here
there isn't anything that would make you want to read on
nothing traumatic
obligatory or accidental
the events surely don't rhyme and they happen every day
    it's just that a few words, a few things made me remember this

do we still need to talk about it?

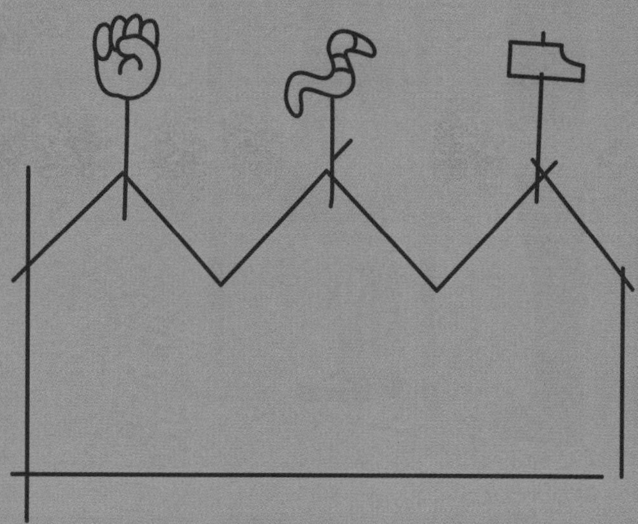

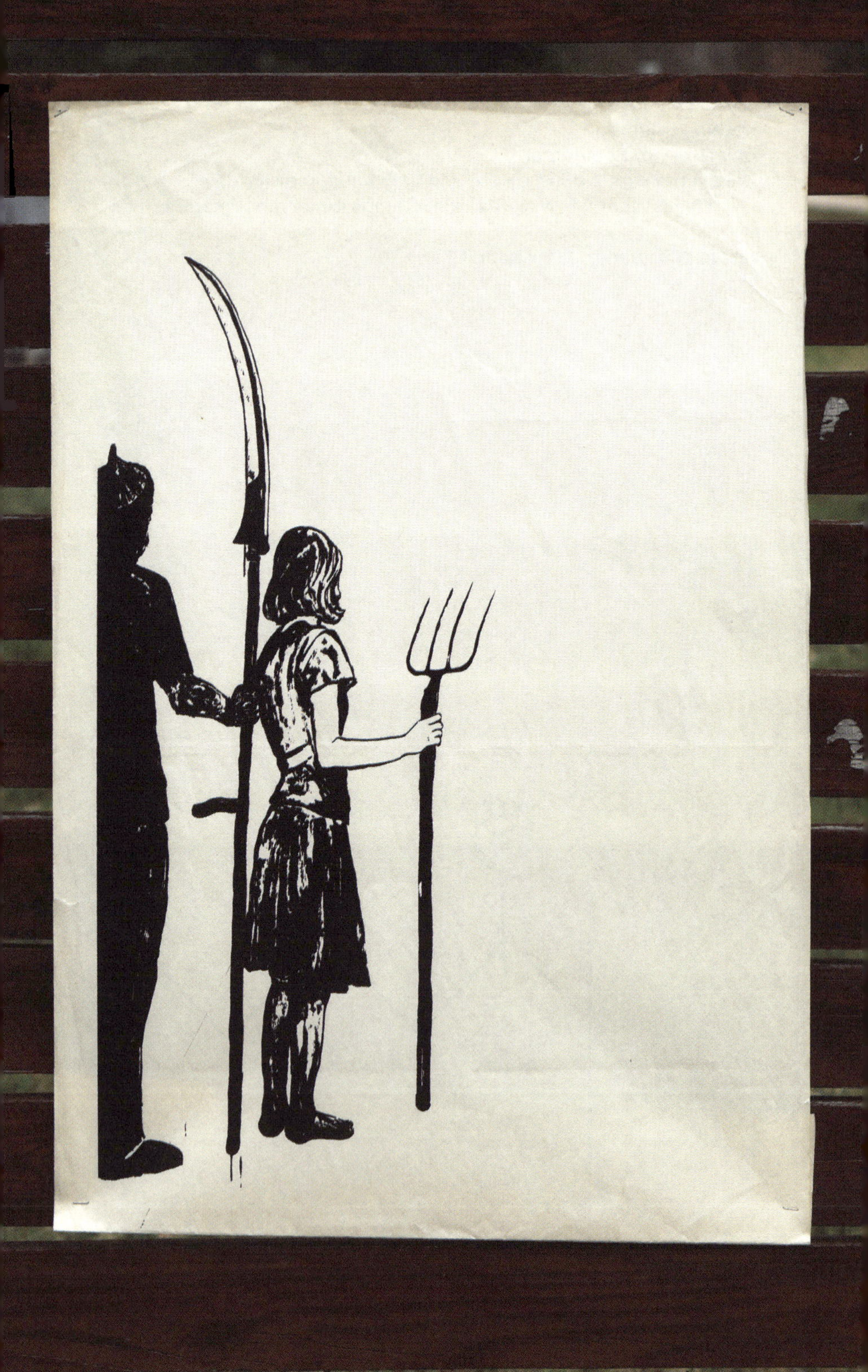

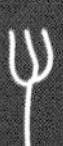

Sci Fi
Agit Prop

Tamás Kaszás

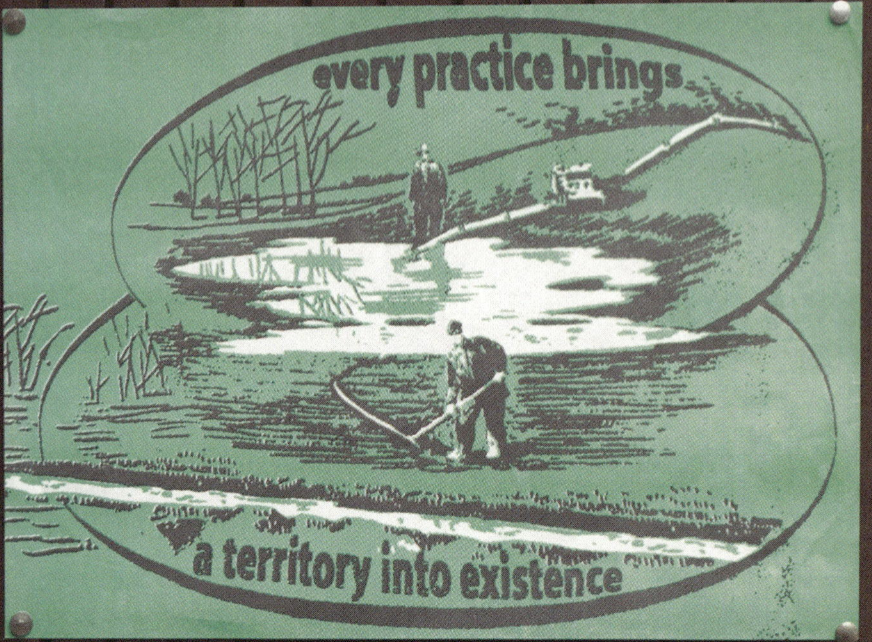

every practice brings

a territory into existence

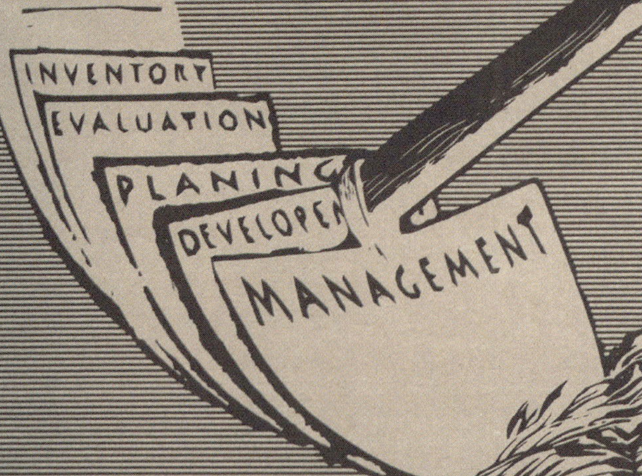

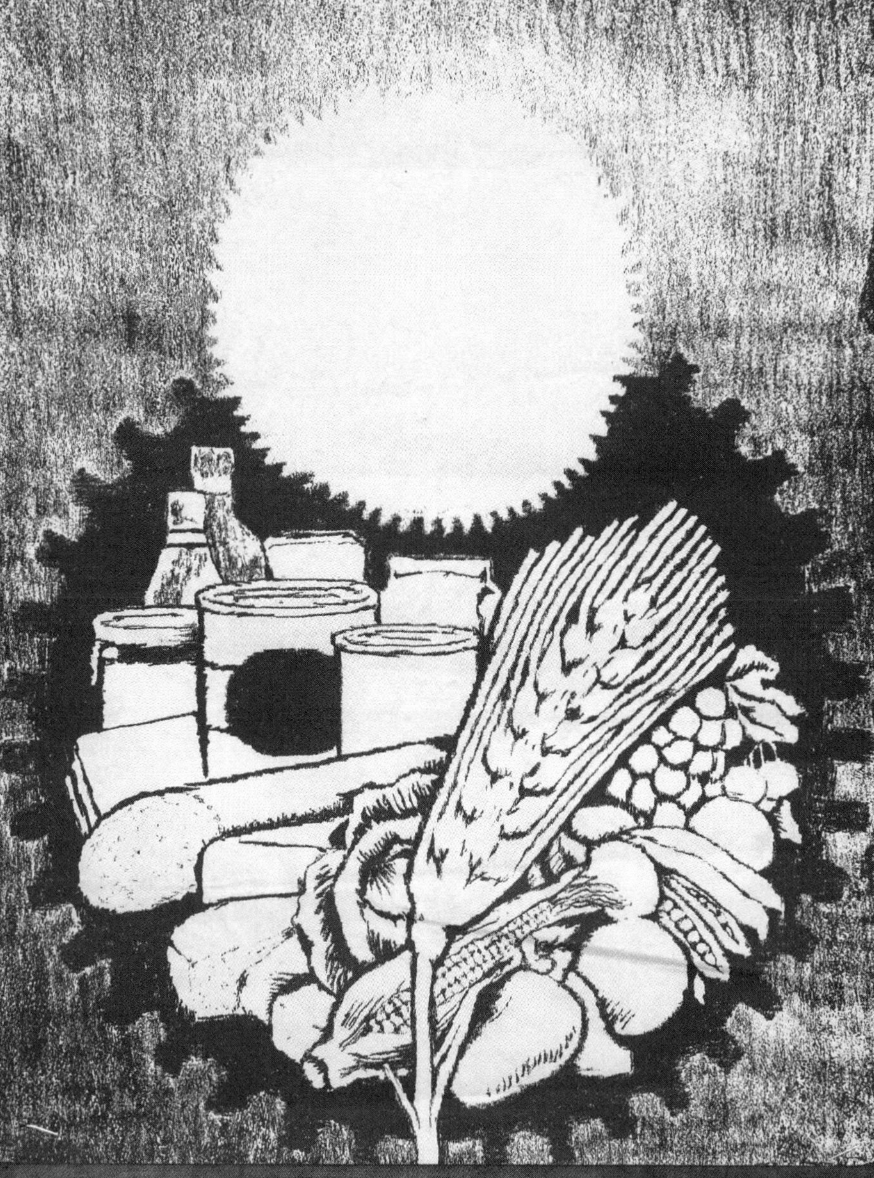
2 percent of the population produce the food of all the others

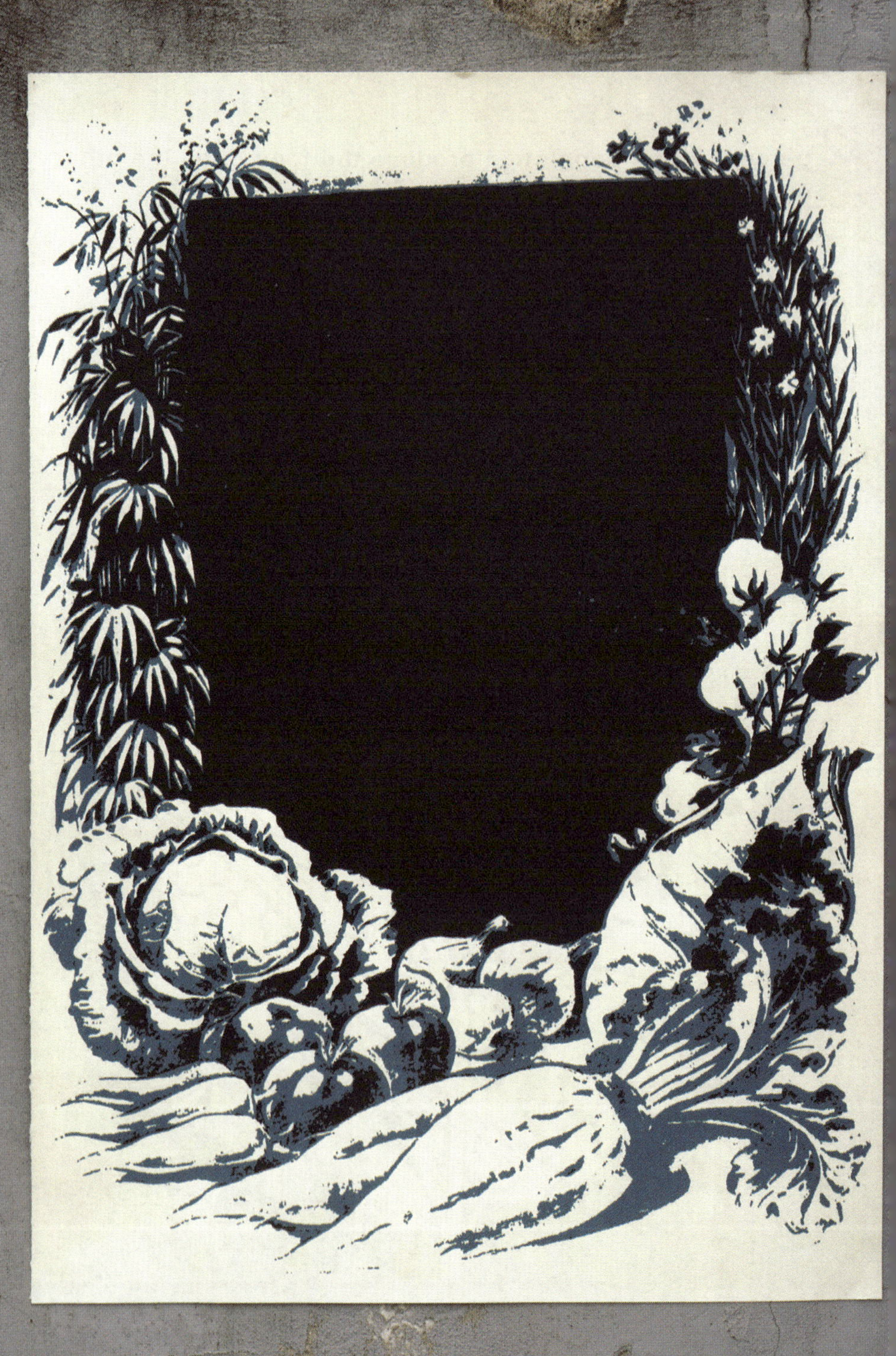

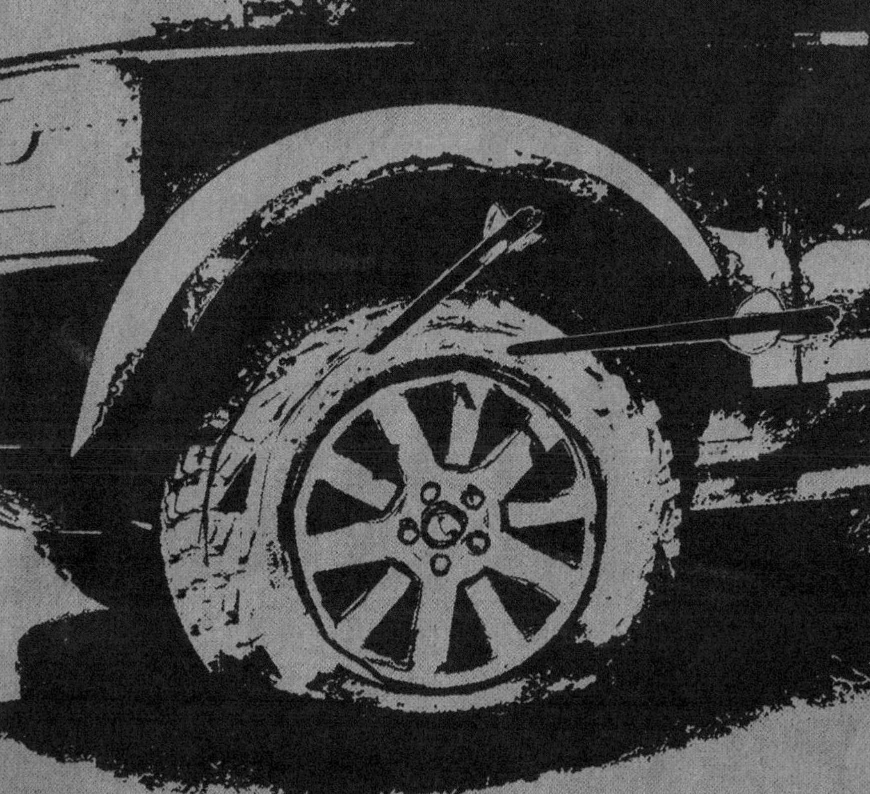
expect
resistance

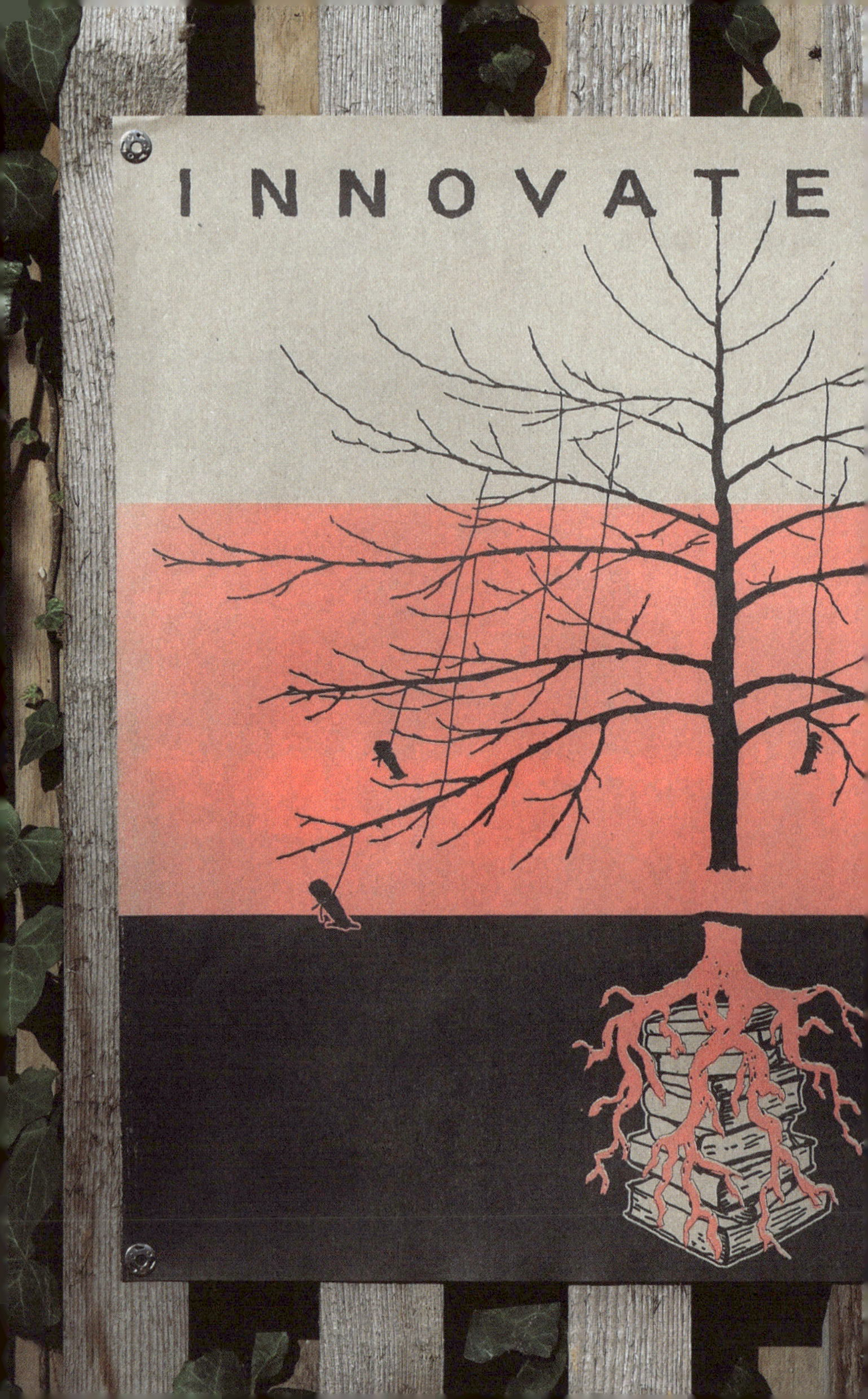

INNOVATE

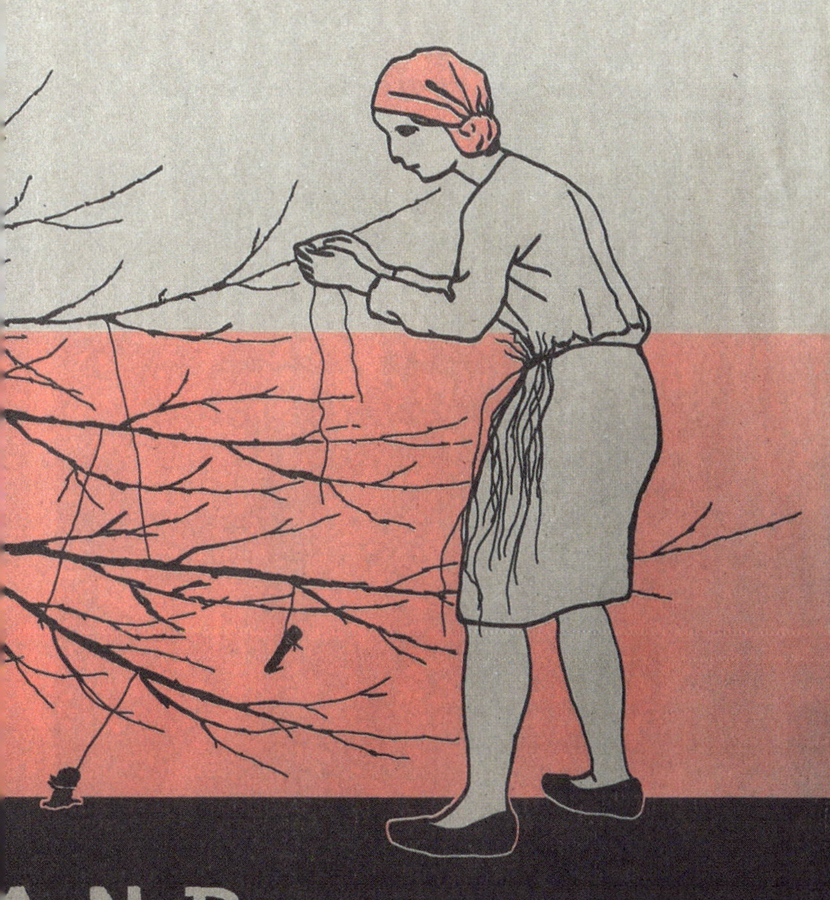
AND
SIMPLIFY

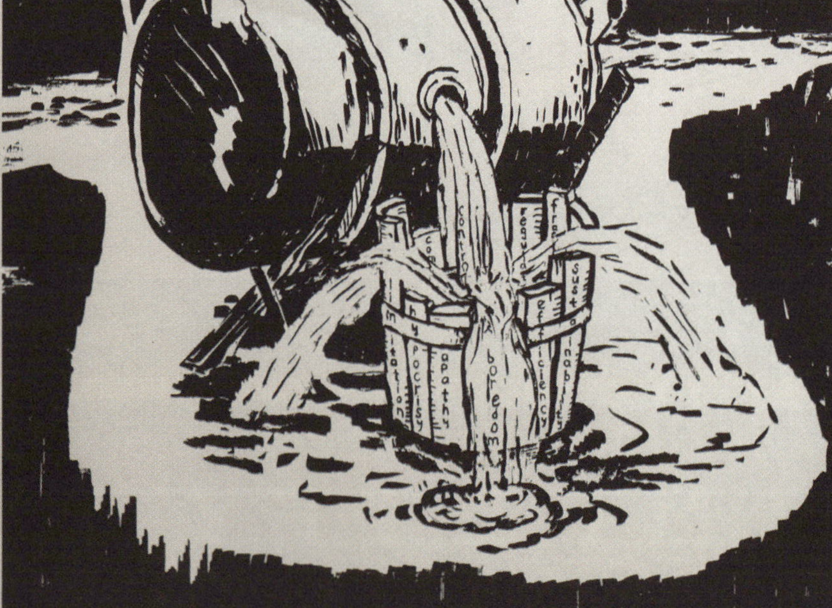
ALL DROPS YOU
WASTE
Time is a limited resource, isn't it?
anyway time is sorrow
apathy
boredom

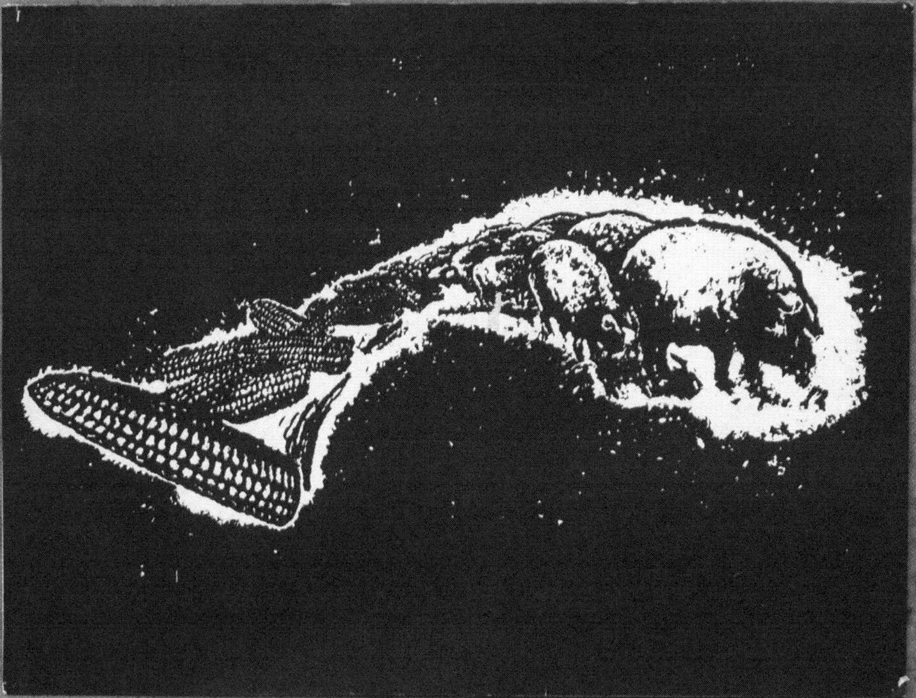

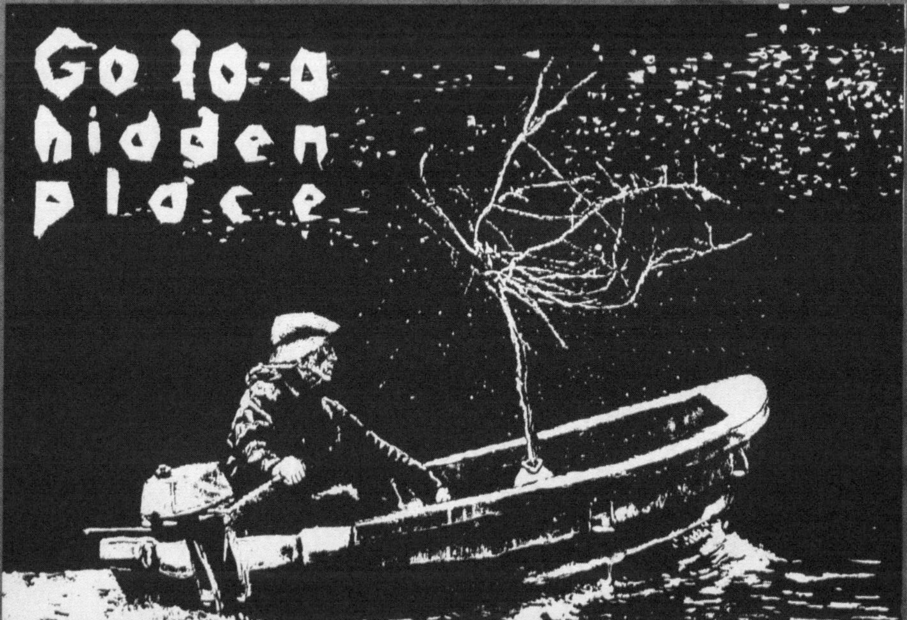

Go to a
hidden
place

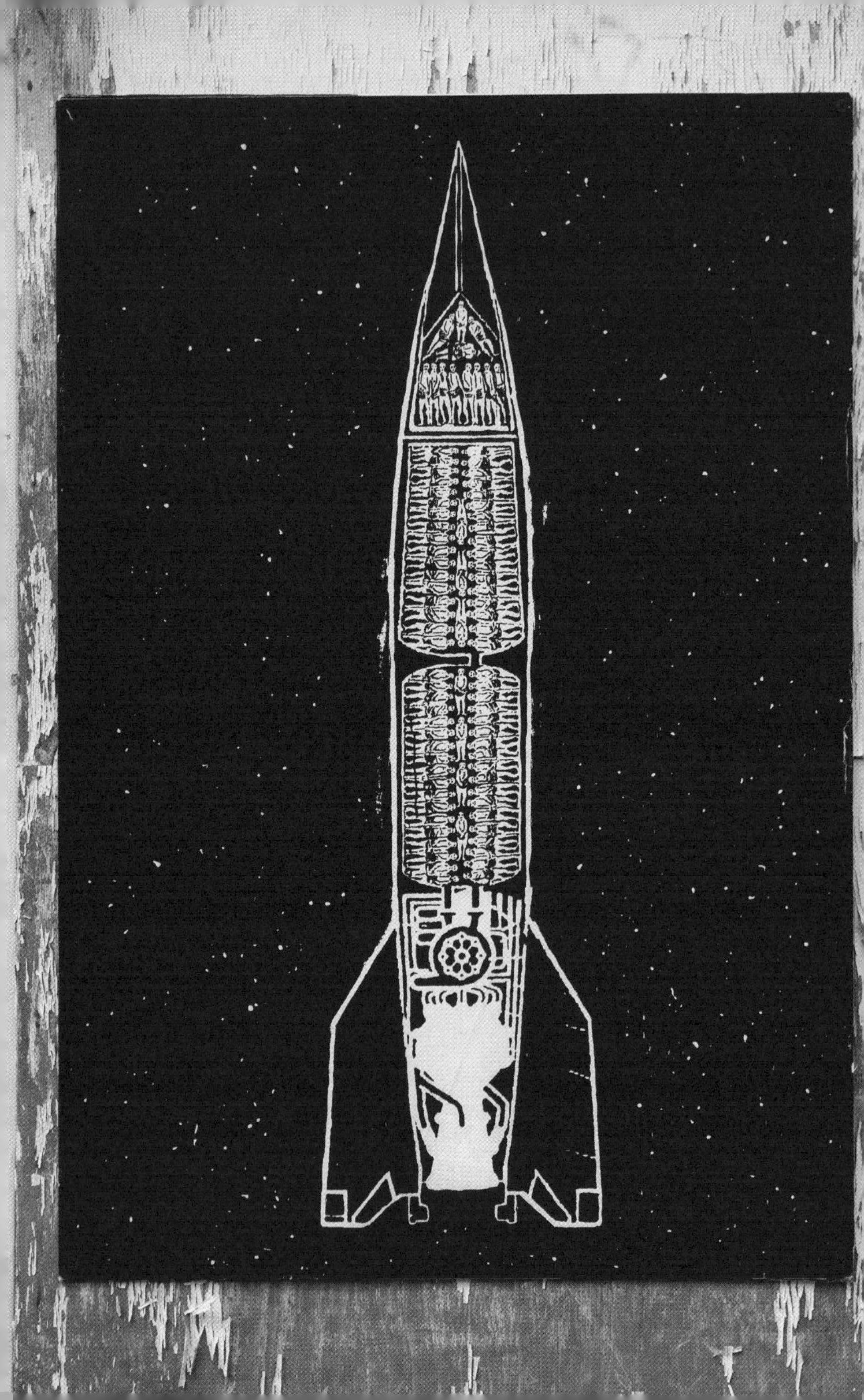

p. 68
We don't ask nor demand,
but we take and occupy, 2013

p. 70
Territory, 2018
Inventory Management, 2018

p. 71
2 Percent of the Population..., 2018

p. 72
Obtain a Yield, 2018

p. 73
Expect Resistance, 2018

p. 74–75
Innovate, 2018

p. 76
Law of the Minimum, 2018

p. 77
New Milky Way, 2017
Go to a hidden place, 2018

p. 78
Space Colonialisation, 2018

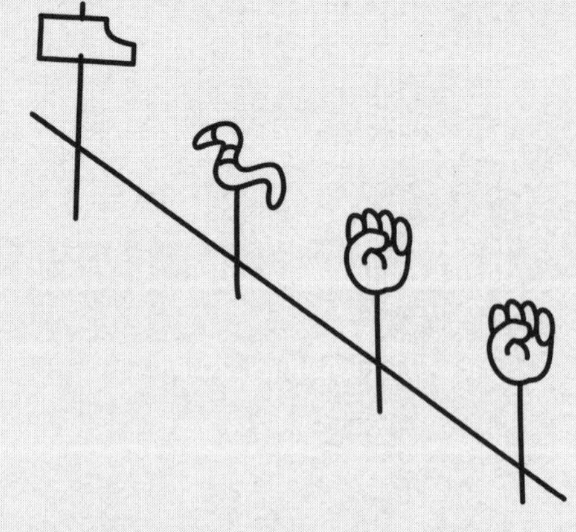

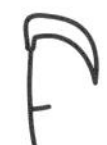

Our Existence is a Resilient Existence: Peasant Movements, Rural Internationalism

A conversation
with
Ramona Duminicioiu .... RD
Fernando García-Dory .... FGD
Alex Toshkov .... AT
and Tomáš Uhnák .... TU

Moderated by
Katalin Erdődi .... KE

The rural realities that the biennale exhibition and the reader deal with are heterogenous, fragmented, and situated, but they are not isolated from one another. How do rural social movements build trans-local solidarities and alliances? The following conversation tackles the past, present, and possible futures of rural internationalism, focusing on Central and Eastern Europe, with the participation of Ramona Duminicioiu, president of Eco Ruralis, a peasant association in Romania, Fernando García-Dory, artist and founder of INLAND, an arts collective and collaborative agency engaged in agricultural, social, and cultural production, Alex Toshkov, historian and author of *Agrarianism as Modernity in 20th-Century Europe: The Golden Age of the Peasantry*, and artist and researcher Tomáš Uhnák, who co-created a new work titled *The Spectre of Peasantry* for Matter of Art.

KE The overarching question of our conversation is how you see the relevance of internationalism in

F rural social movements, and what are the challenges of transnational organizing today, specifically in the East-Central European context? What can we learn from historical examples such as the Green International? Who speaks for whom? Ramona, prior to our talk you mentioned that in Eastern Europe rural people are often represented by urban intellectuals. What are the tensions between representation and self-representation? I believe this also impacts on the question of political identity and subjectivity. What can serve as a basis for identification in rural social movements?

AT In my work as a historian, I trace the moment in which the Eastern European peasantry became a political subject—a force to be reckoned with in the national politics of countries in the region—and how it then projected itself onto the international stage, with all its claims and aspirations. This happened in the interwar period, after the First World War, when the Green International, an Eastern European agrarian international, was initiated by Bulgaria, Czechoslovakia, and Yugoslavia, with Prague as the headquarters of its International Agrarian Bureau. This project was a political failure in many ways, but it has had repercussions.

In his book *The Making of the English Working Class*,[1] the historian E. P. Thompson claimed that the English working class was present at its own making as a political project. Ironically speaking, I would say that the peasantry in Europe was present at its own unmaking... Can we still talk about a European peasantry that needs to project itself onto the world stage? I will problematize this from a historical perspective, but this is also an interesting question today. Is there a possibility of creating

1
E. P. Thompson, *The Making of the English Working Class* (Harlow: Penguin Books, 2013).

a new subjectivity, given the current conditions and context?

RD Romania is the most peasant country in the European Union and one of the most peasant-dominated countries in geographical Europe. We had two main agrarian reforms that gave land to rural people (in 1864 and 1921), but none of these were the result of the political work done by the Peasant Party, which is one of the oldest political parties in Romania. They were the ones who participated in the Green International, the International Agrarian Bureau, and other projects, but in reality, they were disconnected from the peasants. The party was led by intellectuals—urban people.

As we [peasants] see it: what we have is the result of our own work, our struggle, and our model of agriculture, which is also a way of life which is resilient. We have survived on our own, not thanks to any political project or support from the state. In fact, we have survived *despite* efforts made by the state and various political projects. Our existence is a resilient existence.

We are living in historic times—we are experiencing one of the worst crises at a global level—and more than ever, we feel the need to cooperate at a regional level, within Eastern Europe. This hasn't been done before, at least not at a grassroots level and not in our lifetime. There is no group in society who has this experience and who could guide us. It is something we need to build, more or less from scratch. We use some common elements from the past, but the past is also complicated. We must keep in mind: Eastern Europe is not a monolith—we are not the same; there is a lot of diversity within the region. Currently, we are dealing with a full-scale war, and this makes things very complicated. Yet it makes cooperation even more important—it is much more needed.
But we also feel alone in this process; in a broader

F

European context we have not yet found the appropriate way to support an articulation for Eastern European peasants.

TU I can talk about Czechoslovakia/Czechia, which—if juxtaposed with Romania—is on the opposite side of the spectrum. The peasantry is a non-existent entity here. For some time now, I've been obsessed with re-thinking the relevance of the peasantry in the twenty-first century in a country like Czechia, which went through the same or very similar collectivization as Romania, with one distinction: Czechoslovakia—together with Bulgaria—was one of the most heavily collectivized countries in the Eastern Bloc, with up to 98 percent of farmland collectivized. After the Velvet Revolution, the term "peasant" and peasantry as a class was still used, but then it disappeared from societal and political discourse and was replaced with another term. Former peasants became "private smallholders"—with an emphasis on the private—and the Czech term *sedlák*[2] was revitalized and used for "traditional" small-scale family farms. I see it as a big task to investigate who the peasants in Czechia are today and, as Alex mentioned, whether we can

2
During feudalism, most peasants in Bohemia were considered serfs—they had a plot of land and owned a homestead, but they were bound to the land and obliged to work for their feudal lords. *Sedláks* were wealthy or semi-wealthy peasants, whose privileged position derived from owning their own farm and hiring external labor but also from a certain cultural tradition. During the period of forced collectivization in the 1950s, *sedláks* were branded kulaks—peasants who owned more than fifteen hectares were regarded as village rich men and thus class enemies. They were systematically eliminated, and their land was seized. See: "Sedlák," Sociologická Encyclopedie, accessed May 5, 2024, https://encyklopedie.soc.cas.cz/w/Sedlak/.

Editor's note: the endeavor to revitalize this term can be linked to the rise of anti-communist sentiment after the transition as well as a desire to restore the social status of these farmers who strongly self-identified as victims of communism.

still talk about peasantry. Why is it relevant to talk about it? For several reasons, I think.

But first, I want to remind us of the definition of peasantry. According to the 2018 UN Declaration on the Rights of Peasants and Other People Working in Rural Areas (UNDROP),[3] a peasant is any person who engages or seeks to engage, alone or in association with others as a community, in small-scale agricultural production for subsistence or for the market. Peasants rely significantly, but not exclusively, on family or household labor and other non-monetized forms of organizing labor. They have a special dependency on and attachment to the land. This is also the definition used by the international peasant movement La Via Campesina. It resonates with Frank Ellis's definition[4] from the late '80s or early '90s, which said that peasants derive their livelihoods mainly from agriculture, utilize mostly family labor, and are located within a larger capitalist economy. Some scholars object to this last point: for example, Haroon Akram-Lodhi claims that there are no peasants in Europe because—and I'm echoing Alexander Chayanov[5] here—the peasant way of life and farming is an essentially non-capitalist form of organization. But capitalist subjectivity and interrelationality is so pervasive that people referred to as peasants cannot escape these neoliberal capitalist relations; they have to engage with it. This affects their livelihoods, the

3
"Brief History," UNDROP, accessed May 5, 2024, https://www.undrop-implementation.info/undrop.

4
Frank Ellis, *Peasant Economics: Farm Households and Agrarian Development* (Cambridge: Cambridge University Press, 1993).

5
Alexander Vasilyevich Chayanov (1888–1937) was an outstanding agrarian economist, scholar of rural sociology, and advocate of agrarianism and cooperatives both in Imperial Russia and in the Soviet Union after the 1917 revolution. An important theorist of peasant economy, he was executed during Stalin's purges.

way they organize their labor, the possibilities of selling their produce, negotiating prices, et cetera. From a European perspective, Jan Douwe van der Ploeg argues that there is a "new peasantry" in Europe because the definition fits a great variety of practices.[6] Peasantry is heterogenous—this has been researched and affirmed many times. It's not a single form of organization, and it's not very useful to think about it in terms of scale. Rather, one should look at the ways in which peasants organize internal resources (such as fertilizer, manure, seeds) and what kind of—often alternative—markets they form.

In Czechia, collectivized land was returned to its previous owners in restitutions after 1989. Today around 3.2 million citizens—roughly 30 percent of the country's population—own agricultural land, so people still hold a certain power. But they don't farm this land; they rent it or lease it, mostly to enterprises that already operated on vast hectarage during state socialism. The term "peasantry" has derogatory connotations, and it is difficult to find anyone who identifies as a peasant, but I would still claim that there are "new peasants" in Czechia. My concern is that they don't have class consciousness with an agenda and strategy; it's not the rejuvenation of a class as such.

FGD Starting from a more academic-historical definition of peasantry, it is key to understand how it is brought into the political scene as a concept, as an idea—most recently, after the Green Revolution, in both socialist and capitalist regimes. This happens through the alliances and movements of farmers, landworkers, and people working in rural areas all around the world, in response to global food policies coming from the FAO (Food and Agricultural

6
Jan Douwe van der Ploug, *The New Peasantries: Rural Development in Times of Globalization* (London: Routledge, 2018).

Organization of the United Nations) or other institutions after Bretton Woods, like the World Bank or the WTO (World Trade Organization). In the 1990s, small farmers and rural people still made up the majority of the world's population—especially in Latin America, India, and other parts of the Global South—and this had a strong impact on Europe. Claiming the word *campesino/campesina* (peasant in Spanish) with pride is part of a political project. It is influenced by the Theology of Liberation movements in Latin America, where rural development agents confronted the productivist and agri-business policies implemented by World Bank in the 1970s. Emancipatory projects fighting for land reform are often connected with more classic Marxist ideologies—like in the Movimento Sem Terra (MST), the landless workers' movement in Brazil—while others mix different elements. But they all point to the need for an agency to confront the plans to industrialize and technify the countryside that leave mid-size and small-scale farmers by the wayside.

Also, we shouldn't forget about the indigenous communities who played an important role in the articulation of the Via Campesina identity, about the strength of the Andean indigenous peasant movements who brought questions like the mystical to the fore, which became a key element in creating a new identity within the movement. This means not only referring to oneself as an economic, agricultural, or political actor but, as Ramona was saying, as a form of life, connected to other values and other forms of being in the world, in harmony with others, with nature—the notion of *sumak kawsay*, which means "good life" in Quechua. Historically, this connects to movements like the revolutionary socialism of Narodnaya Volya (People's Will)[7] in the late nineteenth century, who challenged the idea that the countryside should be industrialized in order to become more equal.

In Europe, when the French movement takes back the word *paysan*, when in Spain the *jornaleros* (landless farm workers) claim their identity with pride, they challenge the dismissal of the small farmer. In the Anglo-Saxon context, the word "peasant" is still charged with prejudice. The fact that it is being claimed, reframed, and repositioned relates to Jan Douwe van der Ploeg's notion of "new peasants." It's a broad diversity of people and movements.

For me, the question is: How can the sons and daughters of existing farmers (the highly technified farmers of Central Europe, for example) start thinking about their form of life beyond competition, growth, economic productivity, and efficiency? How is it possible to reclaim this identity in an emancipatory way, far from the discourses of the far right, which in many cases fail to represent the anger and anxiety of farming families in Europe. In Spain, we have a far right party—it's relatively new—and it was interesting to see that in the recent farmers' protests, they did not succeed in becoming the mouthpiece for the movement. I think that the farmers' movement, especially the small farmers' movement, knows that it cannot go with any political party. I hope that the discourse will be elaborated within the movement itself and in alliance with other movements at a global level.

RD I want to respond to this discussion about the concept of a peasant. I am a peasant—this is how

7 Narodnaya Volya was a revolutionary socialist organization formed in the early 1880s after the breakup of the agrarian populist movement Zemlya i Volya (Land and Liberty) following the failure of their "going to the people" campaign, with which they had attempted to instigate a revolution from below by organizing the peasantry. Unlike Marxists, they believed in achieving socialism through a peasant revolution, bypassing the stage of capitalism. See: "Narodnaya Volya," New World Encyclopedia, accessed May 5, 2024, https://www.newworldencyclopedia.org/entry/Narodnaya_Volya.

I identify myself, and this is how members of my family have identified historically. I come from a long line of peasants; we were serfs before the last land reform, when my grandfather received land. It's important to keep in mind that what we have in the UN Declaration on the Rights of Peasants is what we managed to negotiate with the governments. In La Via Campesina, we worked for many years on defining our identity, which is much more complex than what we managed to negotiate.

A peasant is someone who is connected to the land, who is integrated in the community, and this has a lot to do with the scale of exploitation, with how they use natural resources for food production. It has to be small-scale because it has to be integrated. A peasant is not someone who engages in land grabbing, pushing out members of the community to create greater exploitation for himself. A peasant is someone who uses traditional seeds and genetic resources, who has a certain level of autonomy. But these are all just elements—it's not mandatory! You can fulfill just one or several and still fit the concept of a peasant. A peasant is someone who decides what food they produce and how. They are defined by diversity and combine various types of food production: they can be fisherfolk, pastoralists, indigenous, landless, or nomadic people. Peasants are investors, workers, land owners. They are very much right-wing with regard to land ownership. In Europe, especially in Eastern Europe, although we enjoy collective rights to pastureland and so on, peasants profoundly believe in and care for the right to private property, as in the right to land. It is not just access to land; it is the legal right to land that ensures protection. When I say "peasants are investors," I am referring to the fact that they rarely benefit from public funding. In this sense, we are among the greatest capitalists on the agricultural stage because we invest our own money—we really are fair players on the free market. We don't deduct our expenses of production from the public pocket like the so-called industrial "investors" do. I know that these discussions about peasants, poverty, and social justice are usually dominated by bloc politics—the left-wing, anti-American, anti-capitalist discourse—but the reality of peasants is much more complex than that, at least based on my experience in Eastern Europe.

Romania differs from other post-socialist countries because in the '90s we didn't only get back the land on paper. It was *de facto*, legally returned to millions of people. After the fall of the Communist regime, this was the biggest demand that people had. Approximately 16 percent of the urban population moved back to rural areas due to this land reform, and today 46 percent of the population still lives in the countryside. My father had a job in a chemical factory in the city, but he moved when his family got their land back. This was his profound desire, and it impacted the life of our whole family.

In Romania we have two dominant food systems. One is the industrial food system run by a small minority—less than 0.5 percent—who control almost 50 percent of the land. They are the rich, privileged farmers, the biggest beneficiaries of Common Agricultural Policy (CAP) payments. They are also the ones protesting today in Brussels and in our capitals. On the other hand, we have the majority of farmers, who produce on up to 100 hectares and represent more than 99.4 percent. Peasants in Romania, who farm less than 10 hectares, represent almost 96 percent of rural people working in agriculture. The peasant model is mostly agroecological, while the industrial model is run by a privileged few who control half of the natural resources.

I want to say one last thing about the farmers' protests happening now. They are not populists; they are actually anti-populist because the people behind these protests are the ones who don't want to give up their privileges. They don't represent the majority of people who do farming in Europe. This is true even for Western Europe. In the EU as a whole, 20 percent of the farmers receive 80 percent of the benefits from CAP. This is a huge disproportion, and the further east you go, the bigger the disparity is.

We are not dealing with populism here—it's a far right articulation. They not only want privileges and money, they are also anti-unionist and isolationist; they just want to close the border. They are anti-Ukrainian and thus against poor Eastern European countries within the economic project of the European Union.

For us, peasants in Eastern Europe, this is very concerning. We need more members from Eastern Europe to join the EU because we need democracy. We can't allow the far right to continue influencing rural populations who have sacrificed so much in this period of crisis. We need rural people to build democracy; without them, we cannot have it. Without vulnerable people, it is impossible to conceive a democratic future!

AT Following Ernesto Laclau,[8] I think about populism as an associative structure—as a "chain of equivalence" connecting grievances in a particular moment, toward a particular goal. If you look back at how agrarian parties emerged in the interwar period, they were also a response to grievances and injustices—different forms of exploitation and extraction—arising from how modernization was carried out on the backs of peasants. The driving force behind the emergence of some form of agrarian identity was the need to address the particular exclusion of the peasantry as the raw material for industrialization—the wealth-producing social layer, which could be taxed to fund modernization—and

8
Ernesto Laclau, *On Populist Reason* (New York: Verso, 2005).

F

the struggle for the inclusion of these people as political subjects.

The conjuncture of the First World War destabilized the ancien régime and enabled the emergence of mass politics. But again, it was a question of bottom-up versus top-down: Who speaks for whom? How do these movements form? In the initial phase of the Agrarian Union in Bulgaria, there was an effort to preserve the party only for peasants—not to have any intellectuals or politicians from the city speak for these movements. But inevitably, scaling up led to professionalization and broader inclusion. If there is a particular conjuncture today in which something can emerge, then *how does one scale?*

Similarly to Tomáš, I struggle with the question "Who are the peasants?" So I look to different theories, such as Eugen Weber's *Peasants into Frenchmen*[9] and how that creates another form of inclusion and a transmutation of identities. There is also something to be taken from the historiography on class consciousness, such as Gareth Stedman Jones's *Languages of Class*.[10] He argues that identities do not emerge directly from material conditions. Rather, material conditions give rise to multiple discourses and formulations of class that appear and then recede within different contexts. The biggest challenge I see is: In which conditions can peasants address this exclusion? In other words, what do they become, what political projects can catalyze the re-emergence of a particular identity, and under which conditions on the global stage is this struggle for social justice or inclusion advanced or impeded?

9
Eugen Weber, *Peasants into Frenchmen: The Modernization of Rural France, 1870–1914* (Redwood City: Stanford University Press, 1976).

10
Gareth Stedman Jones, *Languages of Class: Studies in English Working Class History 1832–1982* (Cambridge: Cambridge University Press, 1984).

KE On the subject of peasant identity as a political identity, I remember, Tomáš, that you once told me that even in agroecological movements, political identity is not necessarily addressed. You mentioned that at the biodynamic farming school you had recently graduated from, there was little discussion about what kind of political consciousness is needed to pursue certain farming practices.

TU This is a very difficult topic, but it is common in the Czech or Czechoslovak post-communist context, where we are still struggling to reframe ourselves as citizens instead of consumers—consumers as passive actors who receive services as opposed to citizens who are active members of the community with rights, a voice, and an agenda. We often hear that "food is political"—this is very present in the Western discourse—but we don't have a translation for this in the Czech context. We have yet to fill it with content.

This brings me to an interesting point. In 2013, together with friends and colleagues, we started the first initiative for food sovereignty in Czechia. We introduced this concept based on the definition formulated in the declaration of the 2007 Nyéléni Forum in Mali,[11] which says that food sovereignty is the right to healthy and culturally appropriate food. But we tend to forget that this declaration is not just one phrase—it's a long document which states what we are fighting against: imperialism, neoliberalism, patriarchy, et cetera. This has never entered the discussion in the Czech context. We have depoliticized food sovereignty and made it about individual, personal choices for healthy living, about building trust with farmers from rural areas based on shared values like protecting biodiversity and

11
Full text of the declaration: "Declaration of Nyéléni," Nyéléni International Movement for Food Sovereignty, accessed May 5, 2024, https://nyeleni.org/IMG/pdf/DeclNyeleni-en.pdf.

so on. However, we need to raise the question of emancipation that Alex and Fernando also mentioned: What do we want to emancipate from? And not only in terms of the peasantry...

My colleagues and I recently finished a large-scale research project in which we mapped how many people are involved in alternative food networks and food self-provisioning in Czechia. This was the first time quantitative research has been done in this area, and we discovered that 77 percent of the Czech population is engaged in self-provisioning, 75 percent in alternative food networks, and 61 percent in both. So we have to ask ourselves: Where is the change? For a long time, we thought that we needed to scale up the alternatives—to go from niche to mainstream—in order to make an impact. Now we have done this, but where is the impact? It cannot be seen on any level, neither ecologically, nor socially, nor economically. These alternative platforms just cater to the needs of the people who can afford them, while the conventional food system is also co-opting and appropriating them; therefore, I am very skeptical about their emancipatory power.

The second thing that concerns me is: From what position are these initiatives acting? I see more and more disparity between urban liberals and rural farmers within the alternative food networks. The ecological concerns connect them, but there is a huge disparity in terms of worldview and political identification. In the most progressive networks, members are leaving because they don't want to cooperate with farmers who are environmentally conscious but also populist, right-wing or ultra right-wing, anti-migration, homophobic, et cetera. They are anchored in completely different social structures, and there is no reflection on this within the alternative food networks.

When thinking about regional cooperation, the first thing that comes to mind is that the most active and fruitful cooperations are between the big players—the Czech farmers' associations who are members of Copa-Cogeca, the European platform for industrial agriculture. At the end of the day, what's at stake is who's got the power. That is why I was referring to the class consciousness of the new peasantry before, because class consciousness could give you the tools and agenda to organize as a movement. But there is still a strong anti-communist sentiment, which doesn't allow us to think beyond capitalism, because "we tried the alternative and it failed." The new peasantry in Czechia doesn't show any solidarity with, nor a sense of belonging to, the more than two billion peasants worldwide; there is no sense of collectively striving for some kind of lifestyle and essentially a political agenda against exploitation and accumulation. Even though 77 percent of the population is engaged in alternatives, there is no self-organizing, no formulation of aims or strategies. So in the end, it's a status quo that helps the corporate food regime paradigm flourish, even though food sovereignty was originally conceived as a way to take back power.

KE Ramona spoke about how we are living in historic times in which—from the perspective of rural social movements—it is essential to have more regional cooperation. What possibilities do you see for this, and what challenges? Fernando, could you tell more about your experience with INLAND and how you see the role that artists and artistic practices can play in such transnational organizing?

FGD I think what is needed, especially in the West, is a cultural strategy that positions the rural and the peasant at the core of a paradigm for change. We need to counterbalance the many years of capitalist or state capitalist propaganda that have dismissed the peasant. I don't think mass media or other

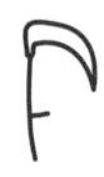

forms of propaganda are adequate languages to develop something so subtle. In INLAND's work for documenta fifteen,[12] the Museum of the Romanian Peasant and its director Horia Bernea were important references for me. Founded as an ethnographic collection in the late nineteenth century, this institution participated in creating the discourse of the nation-state, looking at the folk aspect, and then it was turned into the museum of the Communist Party. After 1989, its new director Horia Bernea, who was an artist himself, wanted to reimagine how a museum could talk about peasant culture.[13] Maybe this can be the role of the artist: to try to create other ways of looking at such questions and to present them. I'm living in a rural context, so it can happen that my neighbors call me to do something for a seasonal celebration. Right now we are building an ephemeral structure that will become a seed bank and a radio station. What we need is to put the artistic languages of the avant-gardes to work in addressing everyday rural life and its challenges.

In recent years, we have been working on a European project called Confederacy of Villages with partners from southern Italy, northern England, northern Sweden, and Armenia. The group from southern Italy, Casa delle Agriculture, is made up of neighbors and a few artists; they are recovering old wheat varieties and building a communal mill. This is their way of preventing young people from leaving the village and migrating to northern Italy. The Lake District in England faces very different challenges; it is suffering from tourism. This is also something we

12
For more about INLAND's participation in documenta fifteen, see: "INLAND," documenta, accessed April 24, 2024, https://documenta-fifteen.de/en/lumbung-members-artists/inland/.

13
Vlad Odobescu, "This Museum Shall Be a Barricade," *Scena9*, February 24, 2017, https://www.scena9.ro/en/article/interview-romanian-peasant-museum-ethnographer. Last accessed: April 24, 2024.

need to talk about: how areas in which peasantry has survived because we were not able to industrialize them—in our case, the mountain areas—are now being transformed by economic policies into destinations for adventure tourism, where people go with this idea of connecting with nature. This is also my criticism of current discourses on rewilding. In places where there are fewer people working the land, a wrong environmentalist discourse coming from an urban context prevails, according to which it is preferable to remove any traces of human community, any human component. They are trying to reclaim a lost ecosystem instead of trying to understand the richness of an agro-ecosystem. An artist has to deal with all this complexity and develop different discourses and works.

RD Fernando, you mentioned the Museum of the Romanian Peasant. I agree that it has some nationalist-folklorist views. We specifically never wanted to organize any events there because we say that we don't belong in a museum. We are very much alive.

Regarding the concept of the peasant, I don't think we necessarily need to use the word *peasant* per se; it's more important that people from rural areas identify with the values of this concept. I do believe that in every country in this world, there are people who identify with the values that define what a peasant is. These people exist and they are in continuous transformation. They can call themselves *family farmers* or whatever is culturally appropriate in their context. In Eco Ruralis, we have an open process for the definition of peasants—I believe all these concepts that we work with need to be continuous and living processes.

Regarding cooperation: there is so much cooperation happening in rural areas, it's incredible! Peasants would not be able to survive if they had to do all the work by themselves in an isolated manner.

F

They exchange work, they exchange resources. Cooperation is very dynamic, and it's very much embedded in rural livelihoods. The problem is that these largely informal and self-organized ways of cooperating have never been brought to light, they have never been articulated in public policies.

Regarding cooperation in Eastern Europe: this is something we started working on more than ten years ago with Eco Ruralis. We were the first organization from Eastern Europe to join the international peasant movement La Via Campesina. To this day, there are very few members from the region. In the last few years, we have decided to focus more on the sub-regional level because we got a bit lost in the broader European scene. We don't have the same experience nor the same demands as small-scale farmers in Western Europe. Their demands are much more economically oriented, and ours are more existential. We believe that we can identify them in a more coherent way if we cooperate and communicate with our neighbors. We've been developing an alliance called BILIM[14] across Eastern and Central Europe, the Western Balkans, the Caucasus, and Central Asia. We included Central Asia because of its Soviet past, which in many ways brings them closer to us. We are using the FAO regional process, the only political process in our region that sheds light on Eastern Europe and Central Asia. Within the EU, cooperation is already set in stone; there's not much that countries can initiate. We are afraid of the future because our countries haven't cooperated with one another for such a

14
Founded in 2022, BILIM is an alliance of organizations from Eastern Europe and Central Asia that are active in agroecology. The word *bilim* means "knowledge" in Turkish and other Central Asian languages. The community brings together grassroots movements, NGOs, and other groups that organize peasants and small-scale food producers, indigenous peoples, academics, women, and youths. See: https://bilim.network/. Last accessed: May 5, 2024.

long time. It's been more than thirty years since we had a space for Eastern Europe to dialogue and share. But that cannot stop us from doing the work. We are very advanced in cooperating with our partners in Ukraine. They are extremely determined because of the horrible reality they are forced to live in. They are reinventing themselves. Ukraine was the only Eastern European country in the Human Rights Council that voted in favor of creating a working group to promote and implement UNDROP, the UN Declaration on the Rights of Peasants. They are facing a life-and-death situation; their human rights—their right to food, to resources—are threatened at an existential level. We want to be part of their experience; we want the social transformation happening there to inspire us—we want to take it home and build on it. Hopefully, we can build on it at a regional level.

Time is not on our side. We are in the worst possible historic times since the fall of communism. Every year there are more conflicts, and this is terrifying. That's why it's important to know each other, to trust each other, and to build solidarity. We must fight against isolationist tendencies, against this wave of nationalism, which is very close to fascism and very much against minorities, against people who are different from you, against your neighbors, against poorer countries who drag the bigger economy down. We need to build solidarity between vulnerable communities because these vulnerable communities—often rural communities—are instrumentalized by the people who work against them. We need to help rural people engage in democratic processes because if they fall victim to the far right, there is no prospect. *We cannot do democracy only with privileged people.* We need to bring everybody on board.

TU For me, Ramona's idea to unite the rural populations of countries that are the most protectionist, with the strongest tendencies toward populist right-wing solutions, is very thought-provoking. I think what we are missing—both in academia and social movements—is a collective theory of change, something that we can collectively stick to. Otherwise we are too embedded in our own national or regional problems and unable to think beyond them. As Ramona said, we share the communist past, the post-communist narratives, but sometimes I wonder—does this help? How does it help unite us? What are we emancipating from? If we want to emancipate...

I am afraid that our day-to-day survival is simply so exhausting that people don't have the capacity to connect with others in a similar position or situation elsewhere. This is something a cultural strategy could achieve...

AT I was thinking of posing a provocative question to clarify what we are talking about: Is this political project more about the restoration of some form of human dignity to a group—to the peasants—or is the emphasis more on addressing the contradictions of the capitalist system? It's obviously not a binary; the two are interconnected.

How did this play out historically within the Green International? It was absolutely a cultural movement. On the one hand, it was about including the masses as equal subjects in the radically reconstituted polities after the First World War, when the ancien régime was discredited for bringing the world to such a state of disruption. On the other hand, this peasant subjectivity was articulating a "Third Way," an alternative modernity between capitalism and communism. The two go hand in hand. If you look at how the discourse was changing in agrarianism after the war, the peasant parties were very vocal in saying that peasants are the producers of food, that they are the ones most interested in peace. This was a clear rejection of any kind of bellicose jingoism.

RD I do think that we are very important in this society. What we live is a reality that has made us all but invisible. Throughout history, we have almost never represented ourselves. Many times, others have spoken for us: urban people, other classes, the intellectuals, the wealthy. We've been called so many names, it's difficult to even call ourselves one thing... If peasants live a good life, other people will be impacted too. It's not just for us; it's for more than just rural people. The injustice, inequalities, and discrimination that rural people have suffered is something that can help other vulnerable communities that do not identify as rural—other minorities. Problems are much more visible in rural areas. You can see your neighbor, so you can see much more domestic violence, poverty, all kinds of problems because the way rural society is organized allows you to do so. We can't protect ourselves and hide behind four walls. I think this can help us show more solidarity. That's why I mentioned the cooperation that exists in rural areas. But we don't really know how to speak about our reality. We don't have a pedagogic or an academic way of articulating our realities for everybody to understand.

FGD I think that's the challenge: What is the politics of the rural, of small-scale farming and the peasantry, and in what way is it different from the politics of other interest groups, especially the conservative ideologies we mentioned? This is going to be crucial.

RD There is another reason why we need to unite and why a movement that brings rural people together makes sense. Rural people work directly with natural resources; we have the capacity to release oxygen into the air and help the whole planet. We are a significant part of the global

F

population, and we have this capacity. In rural social movements—peasant, pastoralist, and indigenous movements—climate has always been a concern. We see the climate crisis being aggravated year by year. We need to prepare as humanity for this crisis because when it hits us, it will be terrible. We need to get organized. Urban people, they can't do anything about this—they can only consume less plastic. But peasants can do so much more. It's a political project, it's a social project, it's everything. A human project, if you will.

It's difficult to predict what will happen, but I don't think that only the bad guys have a chance. I see what people are doing in Ukraine—I'm so inspired by that country! It's not a perfect country; it has a lot of social problems. But they're faced with an existential threat, and this brings out the best in people. I think that the pressure that we are starting to feel so dramatically can force us to see things more clearly—to stop wasting time and getting lost in things that are not helpful, to focus on what brings solutions. Discussions like this are important, and I'm telling you, ten years ago discussions like this were not common. They happen more often now because there is something in the air in Eastern Europe that is driving us to communicate more with one another.

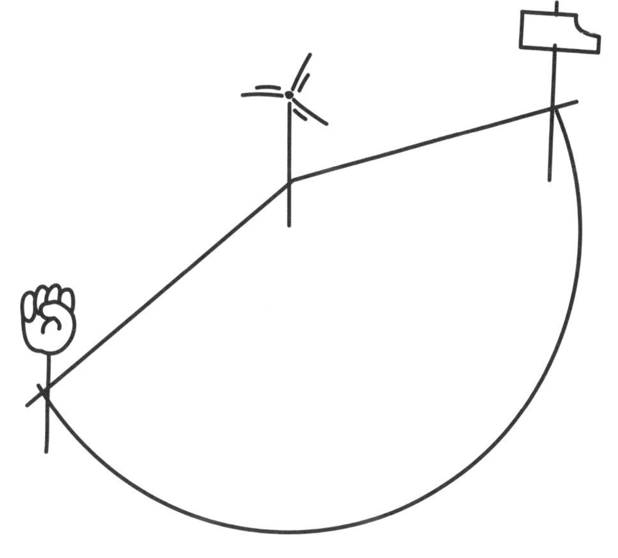

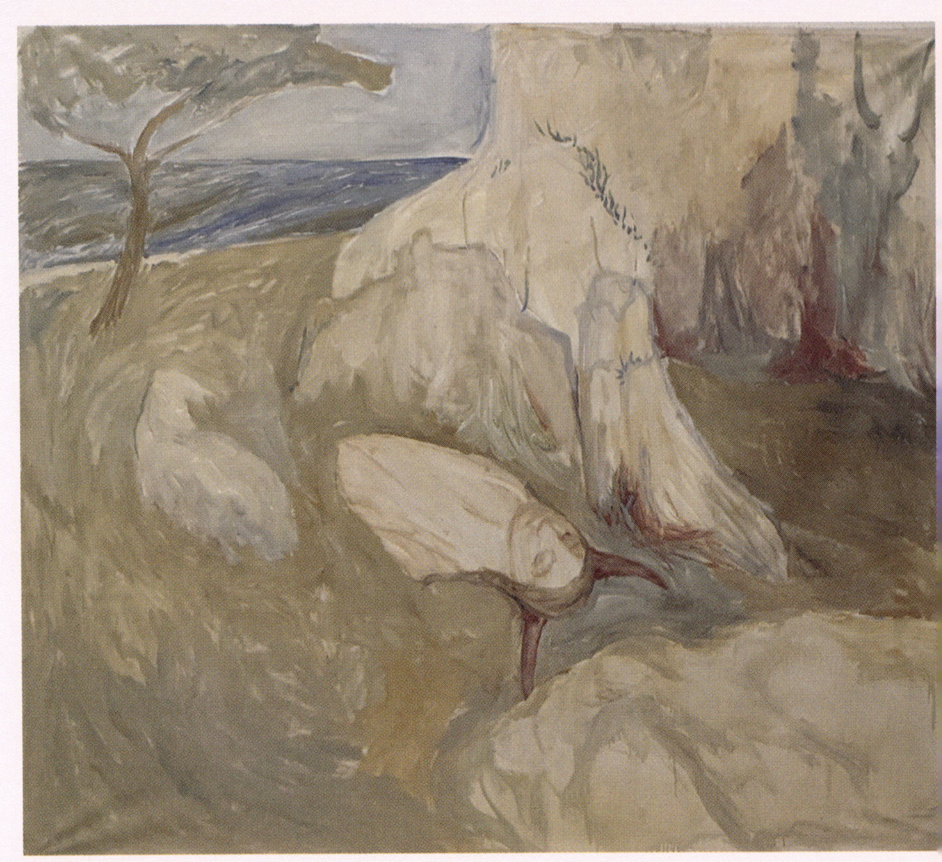

Tyras, 2023

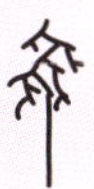

My Dream World Propaganda

Kateryna Lysovenko

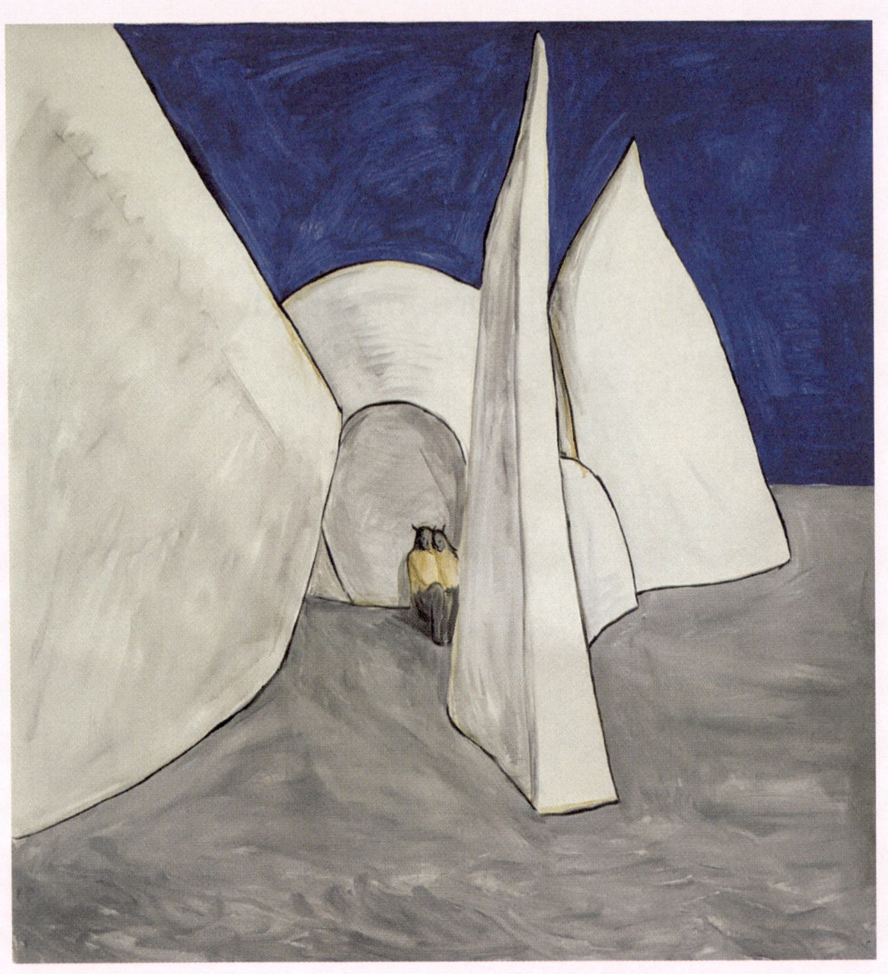

Altar for museum of disagreement, 2023

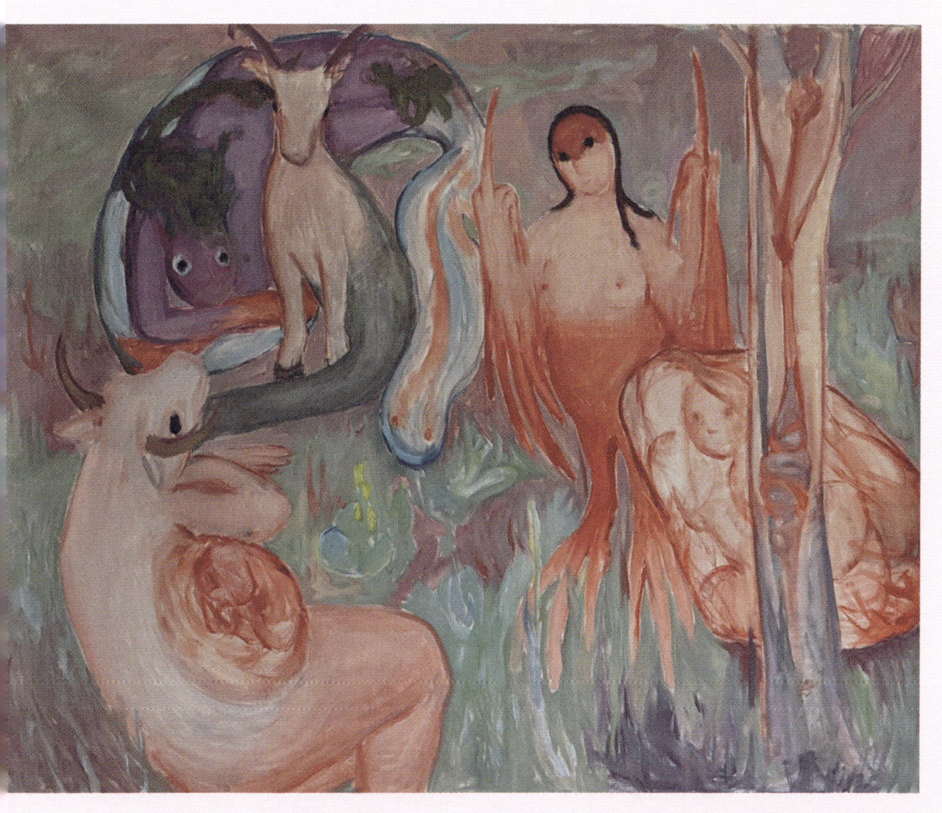

Io from Greek stories, the goddess of water from Armenian stories, the sea goat from Jewish stories, and the woman who became a stream from Moldavian stories, the beautiful Peri from Turkish stories, the living stone from Tatar stories, the tree girl from Ukrainian stories, the stories of people who lived and are living in Tyre, Akkerman, now Belgorod-Dnistrovsk, and a number of similar new and old cities in the northern Black Sea region, are discussing that the past does not belong to empires, 2024

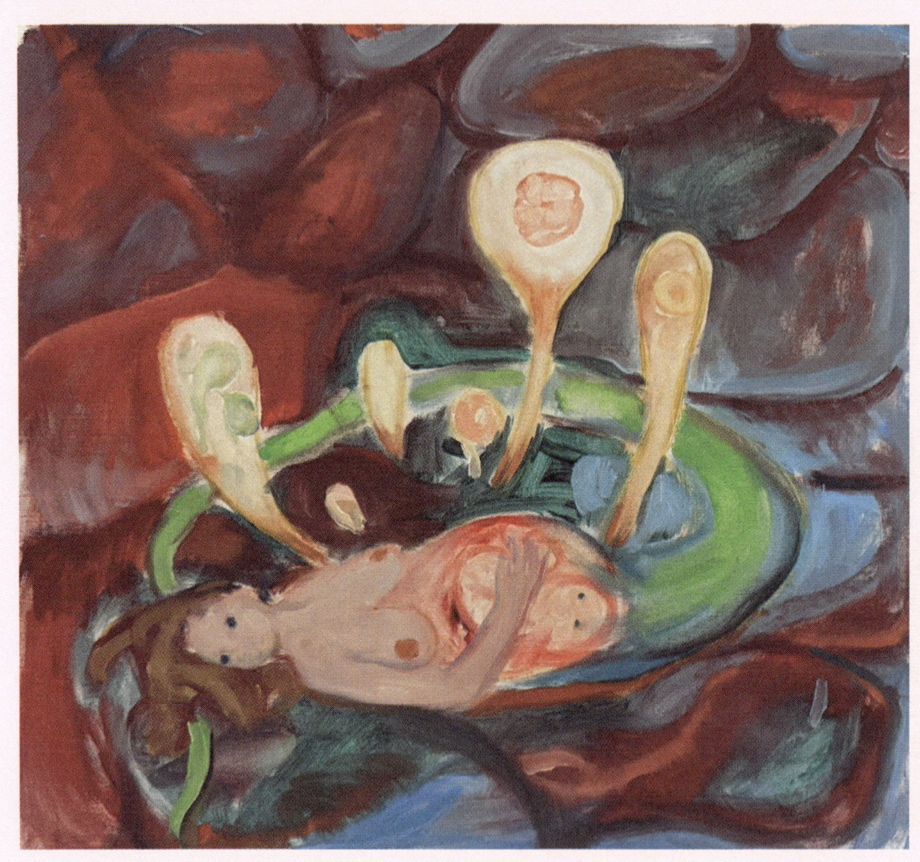

Postmortal child, 2024

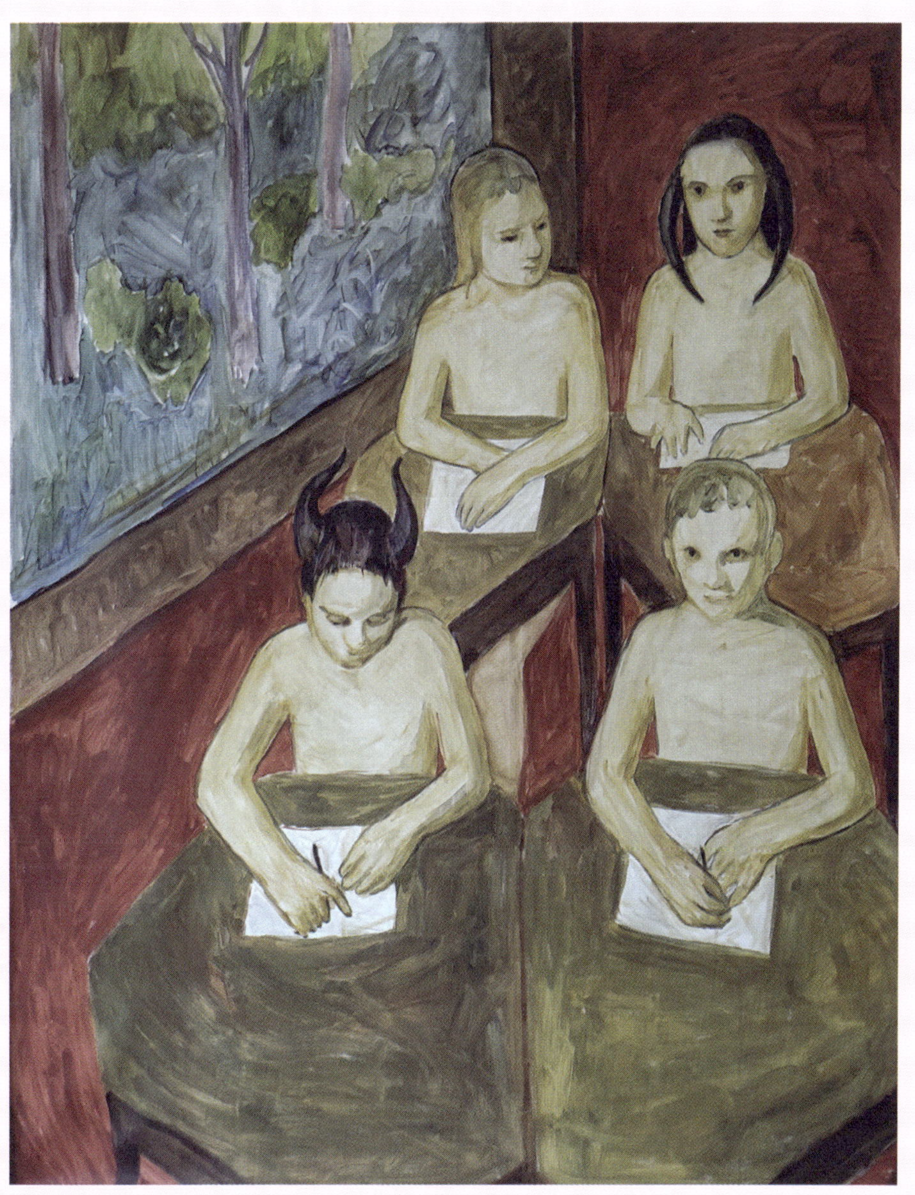

The school, 2022

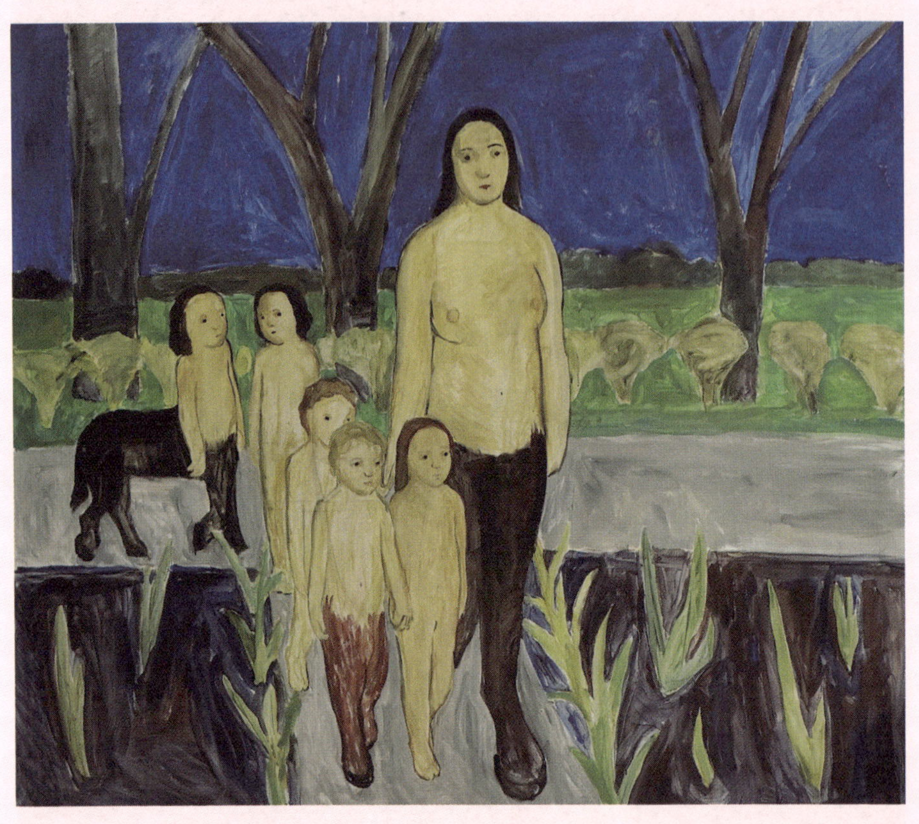

Kindergarten, 2022

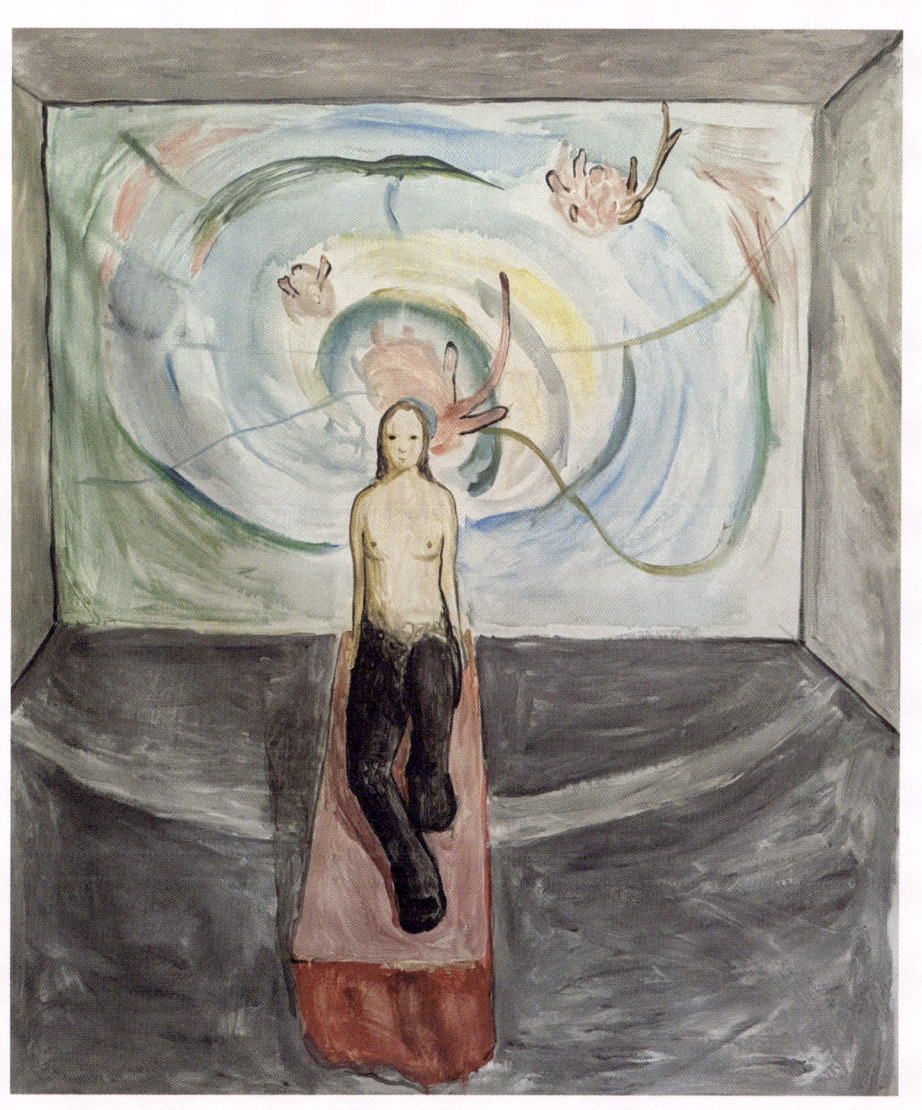

Altar for museum of disagreement, 2023

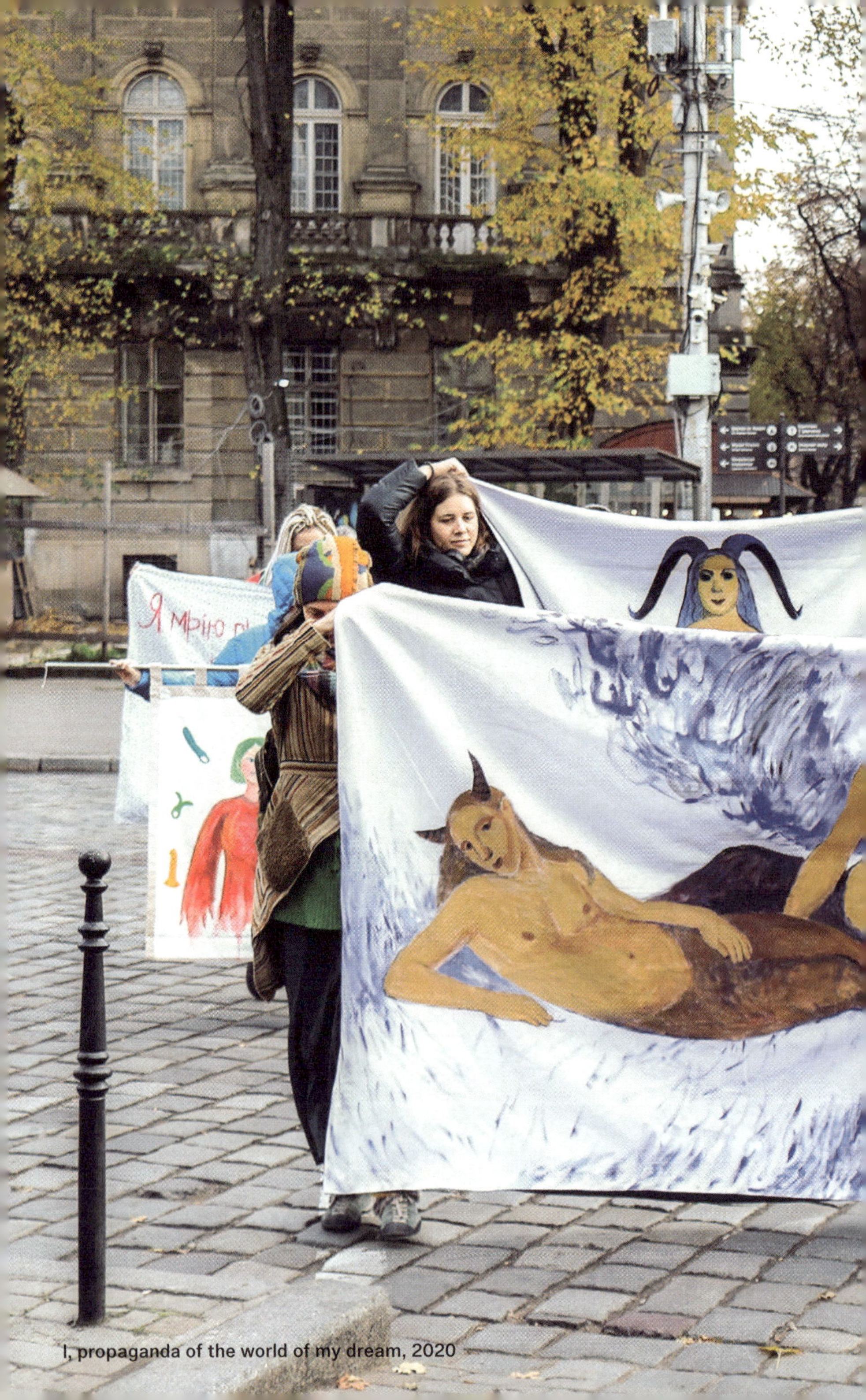

I, propaganda of the world of my dream, 2020

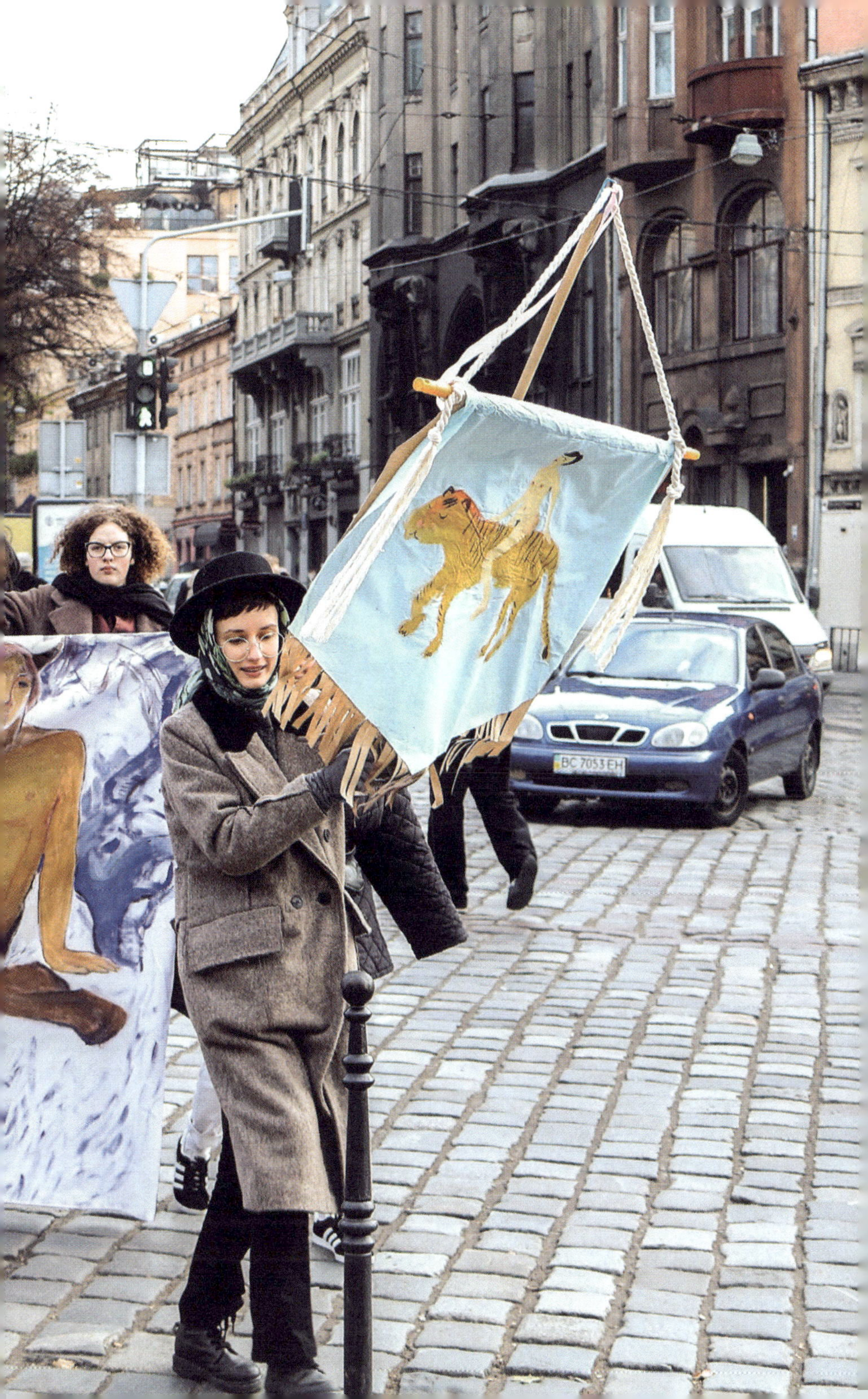
BC 7053 EH

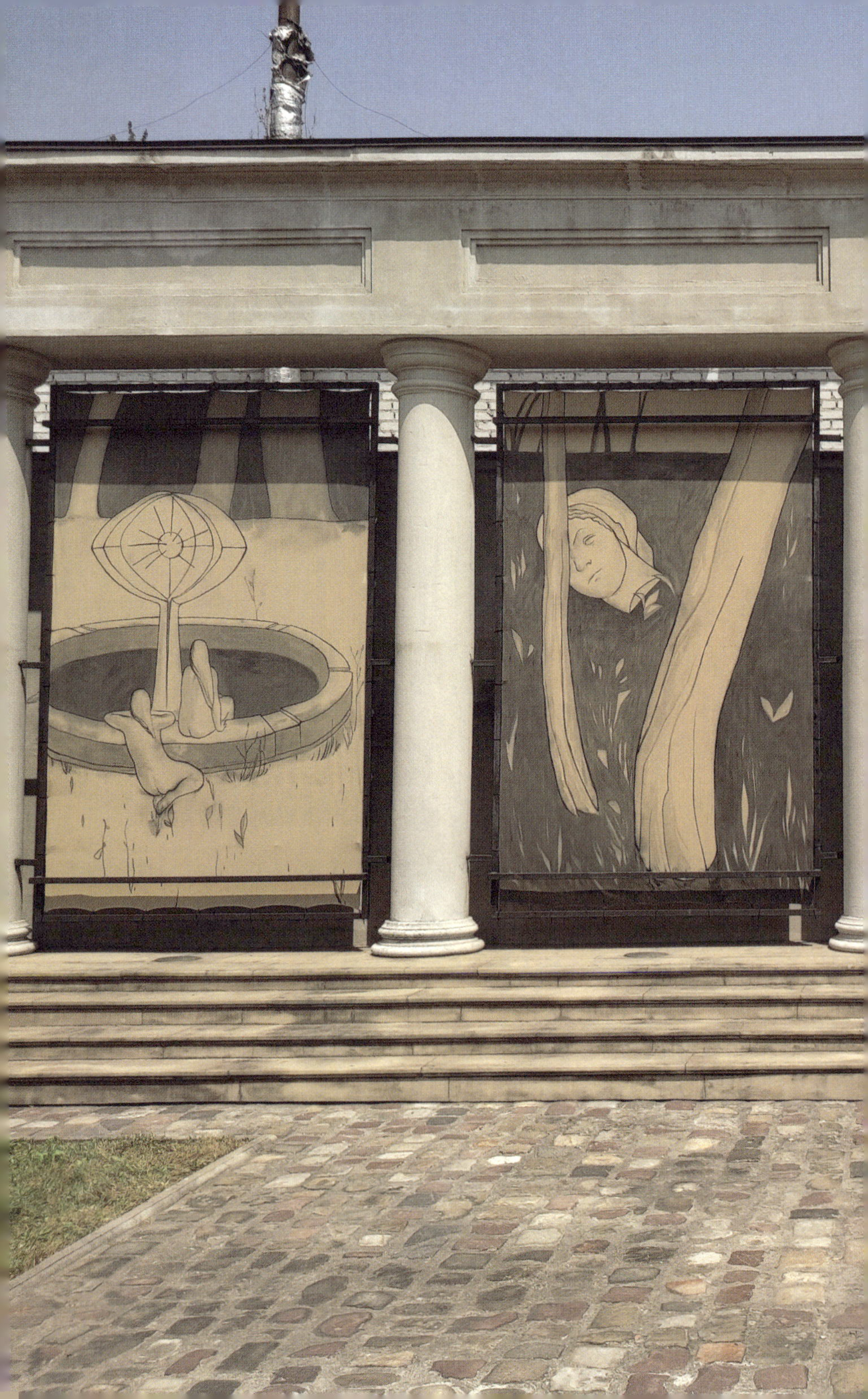

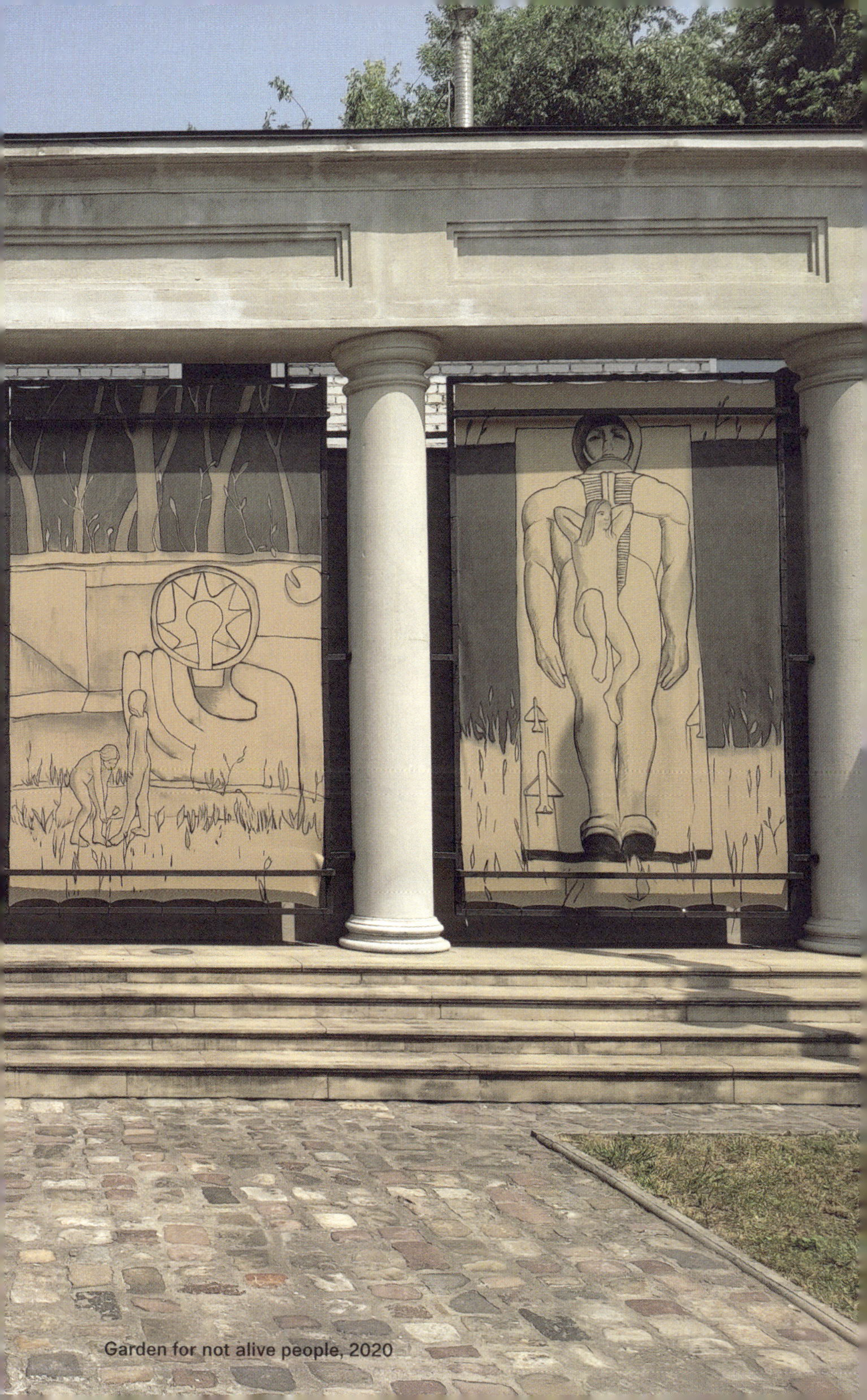

Garden for not alive people, 2020

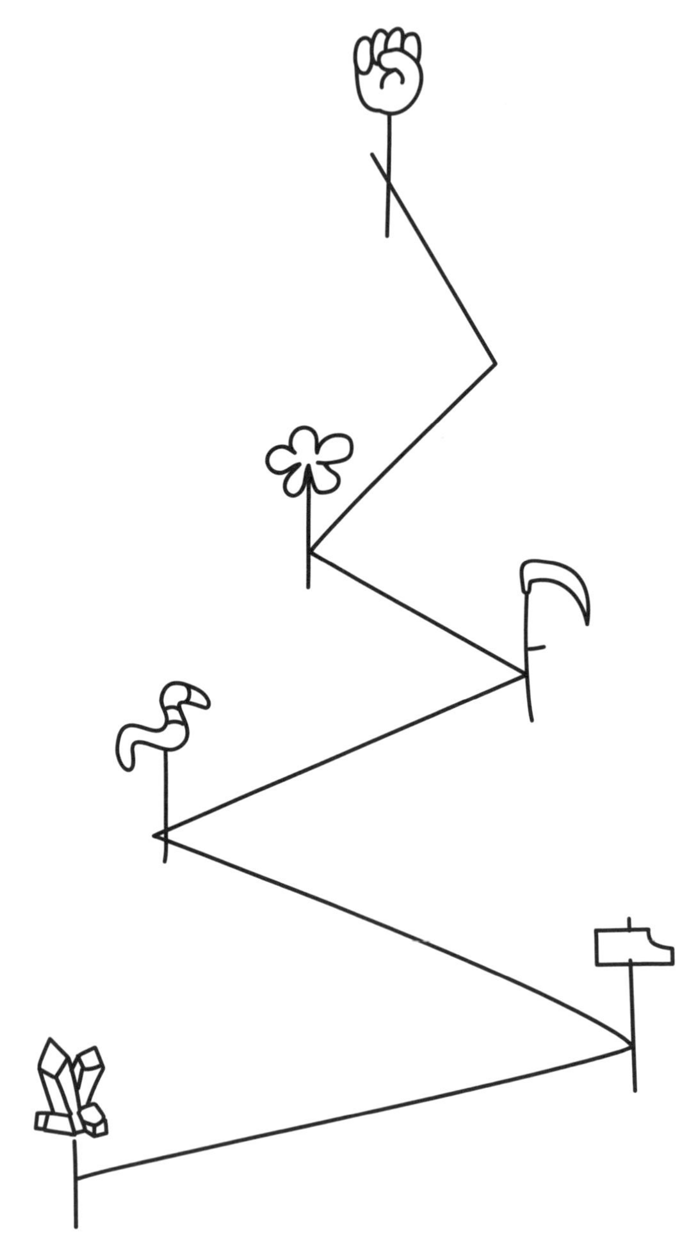

Public Pedagogy and the Toil for Civil Society

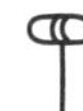

Kateřina Kolářová

The following text is an excerpt from the book *Rehabilitative Postsocialism: Disability, Sex and Race in Eastern Europe*, forthcoming with Michigan University Press. In 2019 the book manuscript was awarded the Tobin Siebers Prize.

Karim identifies as an HIV-positive gay man with experience with substance use and homelessness. I met Karim for the first time on a guided tour of Prague in the winter of 2013. Before meeting him in person, I read multiple interviews he had given to newspapers and media outlets, and as I realized only during the tour, I had seen him perform with a theater group comprised of people without homes during the 2011 protests against the privatization of public higher education. Today Karim continues to work as a guide through Prague, giving his tour companions a chance to experience "Prague's underworld first-hand." The tours are organized by Pragulic, a social enterprise that claims its ambition and objective is to "challenge the stereotypes associated with homelessness by enabling people to experience the world from a homeless perspective."[1] I originally joined the tour hoping to meet Karim

1 The following quotes are taken from the Pragulic website. Some of the quotes from Pragulic reference an older version of the company website that has since been updated. The current website can be found at https://pragulic.cz/en/.

and ask him for an interview about his life with HIV as a part of another project. Taking part in the tour, I realized that this project of "social enterprise" brings home the issues of minority citizenship and rehabilitative pedagogy that I am trying to articulate in this chapter.

Pragulic was founded in 2012 by three students of the civil society studies master's program at the university where I teach. In the first year of its existence, the organization received several awards, among them the 2012 Social Impact Award for its contribution to social integration. In 2014, one of its founders was named Social Entrepreneur of the Year by Ernst & Young and included in the 30 Under 30 list of *Forbes*. Emphasizing the entrepreneurial aspect of Pragulic's model, she noted in one media interview, "I wanted to differ from the NGOs whose financial plan is dependent on public support [...] I wanted a social business more than an NGO with a focus on volunteering." This, in her mind, makes the project more "sustainable" and able to develop as it is not dependent upon irregular and precarious grant support. Yet this also meant a change in the financial compensation offered to the guides, who no longer received half of the earnings of each tour but rather a fixed fee, while the touring customers were also encouraged to tip. "When you are happy with the service in the restaurant, you tip. Don't hold back to tip our guides." The near immediate success of Pragulic and its public acclaim as a business with a praise-worthy added value of social impact and contribution to social change speaks to the marketability of certain forms of "civic participation." And as I elaborate below, it counts on the engagement of minority subjects, to whom it offers an opportunity, however limited, to turn themselves into entrepreneurial subjects, and a model for post-socialist rehabilitation.

Pragulic sells a complex package of multiple opportunities for self-transformation and social change, both to the guides and the customers. It claims that along with allowing customers to "experience Prague through the eyes of homeless people," the tours "give a second chance [to their guides]." Hence, what Pragulic offers is supposedly a transformative encounter in which the guides—people without a permanent home—are tasked with delivering to their customers a pedagogical lesson about civil, compassionate, and tolerant society. They are asked to be “agents of change” who will communicate and exemplify through their own experiences the complexities of the ways in which people become homeless and thus “guide” their customers to an understanding of the social issue and allow them to overcome their prejudices and stereotypes. The Pragulic website notes: “Our aim is to create agents of change, who, based on an intense personal experience, know what homelessness means, who lost all the stereotypes and prejudices, and use this experience and act on it in their further lives.”

Pragulic offers tours led by several *guides*, all of whom list their own profile and life story on the company webpage so that the customers can choose whose life experiences they want to listen to, whose life scenery they want to be guided through, and whose experience should be the transformative force on them and help them shed the stereotypes about people living precariously. At the same time, Pragulic diversifies its experiential education curriculum and, along with the tours, offers other activities to teach people about homelessness. For instance, it offers “experiences” such as “24 hours without a home,” “Team building,” and “Homeless challenge.” With a distinct echo of the ever-so-popular disability simulations such as “blind tours” or “dinners in the dark,” Pragulic too bets on the transformative power of the (as if) first-hand experience: “You can only understand homelessness after you have tried it yourself.”

Pragulic’s pedagogical imagination spans wide to include schools and students as well as corporate businesses and work collectives, offering lessons ranging from ecology to team building to social intelligence. The interactive program directed primarily at students and schools—“The Prague Homeless Challenge”—is arguably drawing on the expert knowledge of homeless people regarding how to survive in the city. The Prague Homeless Challenge claims to want to support “education in the spheres of social awareness, sustainability, and ecology.” In this “city game,” students are meant to learn from homeless people because, as the program's mission statement puts it: "[Homeless people] can survive in extreme conditions because they have learned how to live in harmony with the Earth." Students can learn, for instance, how to sort waste and how to build a makeshift home. Alternatively, they can visit a homeless community or a homeless shelter or partake in "charity" or simpler "fun activities" such as running with plastic bags packed full.

In the other "experiences," Karim and his colleagues' multiple, complex, and controversial histories of precarity, hardships, and perseverance are commodified in the highly ironic offer of the "Transfer of know-how from the field of homelessness into everyday corporate practice." The website describes the activity as follows:

> The teambuilding is primarily aimed at managers and employees from the corporate sphere. It has the form of a structured homeless pentathlon in which the participants can learn from somebody they would never have expected to learn from; they can pick up a lot of practical skills applicable in their everyday work. The aim is to show that a company training may be active and fun and at the same time it can introduce corporate social responsibility (CSR) as a strategic concept naturally penetrating all the functional areas in the company. You can look forward to original and meaningful team tasks in the area of marketing, sales, finance, and human resources. To give an example of a "sales activity," the participants are required to sell directly on the street what they have found in garbage containers and to do that as quickly as possible for the highest price. In case of "finance activity," the team shall use creative team fundraising in the form of street art. In the logistic part, the participants spend the money they earned on food and other things they consider useful for the homeless; those things are later taken by the team to a specific homeless colony.

“Experiencing the Prague underworld first-hand” is how Karim themes his “guided tours” of Prague. He takes his “tourists” through parts of Prague with a history of street sex work and drugs and other economies labeled “criminal.” He tours through places and histories he ambivalently claims as his own. In his commentaries, Karim redrafts the present geography of the exceedingly gentrified and “cleaned-up” center of the metropolis by looping backwards in time and overlaying the present with visions of the seedier past of the early post–Velvet Revolution years of the 1990s. Karim would recount where he and his colleagues in the sex business worked and where drugs were sold. On the tour I joined, he pointed out the hotel balcony where he, in his words, locked his German client out after he told Karim about his seropositive status following unprotected sex. Karim links his own HIV status back to this man. This all is an impromptu performance built out of a hard life. After all, Karim is a proud performer and an actor, and his performing skills are what secure his livelihood and have made him into a sort of sought-after celebrity.

There seems to be more to this, though. In Karim’s words, this is his strategy of “a little shock therapy.” Giving a twist to the neoliberal slogan[2] that shaped the period of “transformation” when he was hustling the streets, Karim transforms it into what he sees as a lesson in tolerance. He believes that he shocks his audience into recognizing “that today [...] anyone, at any moment, can end up [on the streets] without choosing [such a fate].”[3] Karim’s story highlights how he survives and makes a living by reappropriating the commodified “narrative” in an exemplary embodiment of the post-socialist *homo economicus*. There are so many contradictions that he inhabits in a way that allows him—barely, but still—to survive. One of Karim’s many talents is to turn himself into an entrepreneur of himself, cleverly commodifying his past to stay alive in a present that remains precarious.

2
Naomi Klein, *The Shock Doctrine: The Rise of Disaster Capitalism* (New York: Metropolitan Books, 2007).

3
Karim, personal communication with the author.

Turning his life story and himself into spectacular performances that genially reflect the audiences' desire for particular stories and—as I witnessed during the tour—into a spectacle of the untold stories of the post-socialist "transformation" that offset the audiences' "successes" at managing to craft comfortable and more livable lives than his is a strategy that is part of what secures his survival. Karim loves to attract attention. He knowingly and deliberately juggles the everyday performances of gender trouble, turning himself into, as he says, "a spectacle." However, these performances of a spectacle are a deliberate part of his concept of educating the public, which goes beyond the social pedagogy outlined by Pragulic and challenges homophobia, AIDS-phobia, and gendered ableism. His performative presentations and gestures of campy diva exaggerations loop in time and overlap the present with past, the acute with the chronic. Karim elabors the time of a special geography, his life, and the imagination of his audience. Most importantly, these guided tours, where Karim is part of the exposition that is being explored and shown, give him time. Karim turns his past failures into social and economic capital, and he regains his agency by doing so.

Kryštof is an HIV-positive gay man with a life history similar to Karim's. He too was homeless for long periods of time, lived rough, and has a history of substance use. Last time we spoke, several years ago, Kryštof told me he had a very busy work life and was engaged in several art and public outreach projects. On this occasion, we mostly talked about his engagement in Živá knihovna (Living Library),[4] a project initiated and run by the Czech branch of Amnesty International. Amnesty International frames the Living Library as an educational project focused on preventing "discrimination, racism, xenophobia, and extremism," all of which is captured in the motto of the program, "Through reading to openness," where reading means meeting actual people who volunteer to be "read" and to share

4 The website of the Czech branch of Amnesty International no longer contains active links to the Living Library.

5 Kryštof, personal communication with the author.

their life book/stories with their audience. "Instead of typical books, in Living Library, students can borrow [sic!] people or living books. Even living books can be read—through dialogues and the sharing of life stories." Readers who enter the Living Library can "borrow" a "book," who will tell them stories about the life of ethnic minorities in the Czech Republic, stories of refugees and migrants, people with disabilities, people "with a minority sexual orientation," with a "minority religious creed," people with experience using drugs, and homeless people. Amnesty International, like Pragulic, believes in "working to break down preconceptions and stereotypes" and to improve the relationship between the "majority" and "minorities":

> [The Living Library] is unique mainly because [...] [it offers] a space for open dialogue, [...]. The mutual encounter helps to dissolve the barriers to communication between representatives of the majority society and [...] minorities and in contrast supports their mutual relationship. The [Living Library] gives students the opportunity to meet someone in their ordinary lives they would probably never meet. [...] This approach makes it possible [...] to reflect on questions of discrimination, social exclusion, extremism, and racism in context and based on personal experience.

Kryštof takes great pride in being part of the Living Library and in the fact that, in his words, his "book of life" bridges a wide range of genres: "[I represent an] artist, actor, HIV-positive, and homeless person. [My book] includes [stories] of seropositivity, criminality, travesty... life on the street... [I am] an encyclopedia of a kind... I embody more stories than other people."[5] The pride that Kryštof expressed at being "an encyclopedia" is grounded in the notion that his "book of life," precisely because it encompasses a more varied range of chapters and experiences, is especially valuable (and more valuable than those of other people) as a resource for challenging social stereotypes and—importantly—for teaching tolerance. As Kryštof understands, his experiences, so rich in precarity, adversity, and hardship, are converted through the Living Library into valuable capital in the collective project of creating a more tolerant society as well as into a sort of social capital, albeit of questionable value for someone precariously positioned like himself.

Similarly, talking about his own work as a guide, Karim keeps coming back to emphasize that he loves this work because it allows him to inform people about homelessness and change their perceptions of people living on the streets. It is most of all because he believes that, in this way, he is making people and society more tolerant and accepting of people living in precarious housing, people setting up provisional homes in public spaces, people who work as sex workers, people who take drugs, and/or people living with HIV. He says, "I am calling attention to HIV, prostitution, sexual orientation, and other issues that still have not gained social tolerance."[6] Kryštof's and Karim's words echo each other; they both accentuate the value they see in their engagement with the public or the "majority." They both frame their work as laboring towards a more tolerant society, towards social diversity, and towards reduced discrimination and social exclusion. They understand their work (or their commitment) both as their civic responsibility—because as minority members they have a particular and teachable experience—and as a form of public pedagogy teaching tolerance, teaching towards an open and civil society.

When I last met Kryštof, he was still living very precariously, overstaying the length of time a person is allowed to live in supported housing, looking at very real possibility of needing to leave soon. As his situation suggests, people like Karim and Kryštof, who are dedicated to these forms of "public pedagogy" often have few options outside the limited space of those projects which are recognized as valuable because of the "pedagogical lessons" they offer for the majority. What does it mean, however, that they use up the life force of the marginalized subjects while simultaneously locking them into such social projects?

6
Karim, personal interview.

To conclude, Kryštof's and Karim's stories frame the discussion of the mythological function of the notions of an open and civil society that were seen not only as the opposite to the totalitarian socialist past but also as a tool of rehabilitative treatment for post-socialist society and were thus associated with the promises of a tolerant and liberal society. As I emphasized above, both Karim and Kryštof retain an understanding of their public coming-outs and engagements as affective work towards "humanizing" the public; they understand themselves as participating and contributing to a tolerant, open society. Yet their existence remains precarious. The mythology of an open society or civic democracy creates a demand for spaces in which to encounter difference, but it also puts the brunt of the affective labor on the subjects marked with said difference. The Living Library project highlights and foregrounds some of the principles upon which the notions of an open civil society rest, while also making it very explicit the amount of labor and investment that is required from the "different life" that is supposedly the focus of such projects.

This opening chapter focuses on the paradoxes and ambivalences embedded in the imaginary of the post-socialist society and the public. As such, it foretells many conflicts explored throughout the book. In particular, the discussion of civility, openness, and tolerance seems to clash with the two closing chapters, which delve into the current manifestations of the ugly faces of post-socialism (e.g., nationalism, xenophobia, homophobia), which are recognizable and recognizably bad both to the national and transnational players. I have argued here, however, that the lessons of open and civil society that post-socialist societies were to emulate in order to fulfill the expectations of "transformation" brought with them the unresolved issues of social hierarchy and inequalities that mark democracies beyond Eastern Europe. These only stood out more clearly and bloomed with unrestrained clarity when introduced and recreated on the heels of the post-socialist upheaval. For instance, the idea of the social that the post-socialist ideologues put forth rejected social equality as a dangerous "chimera" and even compared it to the danger of totalitarianism. Karl Popper's deliberation on equality and the social hierarchies that stood as a major inspiration of the Czechoslovakian political imaginary in the 1990s was interpreted as follows:

> Open society does not [...] *guarantee equal opportunities to all; it is not a classless society*. Its class structure, however, reflects the general rules of social stratification and the fact of high mobility [...], [open society] prohibits the emergence of class-consciousness and thus the emergence of class in the Marxian sense. These only emerge in closed societies.[7]

Furthermore, the main thesis here is that the rehabilitative scripts of transformation relied on utilizing the minoritarian subject to articulate and imagine its own curative "openness" and "tolerance" towards the sexual, racial, or disability difference. This form of relating to "minoritarian subjects" created significant repercussions for the minoritarian subjects and has equally influenced the current discourses that position minority identities as a danger to national statehood. My discussion of the pedagogical and inspirational role ascribed to HIV-positive people or the colonization of the pain of the violent histories of attacks against Roma and Sinti for the rehabilitation of the white Czech nation reveals them as gestures

7
Karl Popper's definition of open society deeply influenced the discussion of liberal democracy in early 1990s. *Reflections on The Open Society and Its Enemies*, which was officially published in Czech in 1994, saturated discussions about the future development and transformation of post-socialist societies. Though originally conceptualized in the 1930s in reaction to the rise of totalitarian national socialism in Germany in the aftermath of WWI, Popper's opposition of "open" and "closed" societies was easily refashioned to fit the post-socialist political landscape defined by the socialism/capitalism binary. For instance, the definition of an open society that appeared in the first post-1989 edition of *Velký sociologický slovník* [The big sociological dictionary] in 1996 leaned heavily on Popper. Emphasis in quotation added; "Otevřená společnost – názory studentů." *Listy* 27, no. 5 (1997): 31–34.

upholding hierarchies and the "violence of value" that makes these "minoritarian lives" only conditionally valuable—that is, valuable only as enrichment to the national transformation.

In this sense, my discussion is in conversation with feminist queer and crip critiques of the neoliberal dealings with difference based mostly in discussing the processes of governance in Western/ized contexts. For instance, Antke Engel's concept of "projective integration" that "fosters individualization and distinctiveness in order to motivate people to actively work themselves into the established socioeconomic relations"[8] is very helpful in linking praxes developed by Karim or Kryštof to practices of neoliberal governance that sprang into existence beyond Eastern Europe. The material that I discussed here spanning from the 1990s into the late 2010s illustrates the negotiating of difference "as threat" and "as promise" or capital[9]—and importantly illustrates that these understandings of difference have coexisted and overlapped across the post-socialist period.

8

Antke Engel, "The Surplus of Paradoxes: Queering Images of Sexuality and Economy," in *Social Inequalities & The Politics of Representation: A Global Landscape*, ed. Celine-Marie Pascale (Thousand Oaks: Sage, 2013), 176–188; here 178.

9

Engel, "The Surplus of Paradoxes"; see also Antke Engel, *Bilder von Sexualität and Ökonomie: Queere kulurelle Politiken im Neoliberalismus* (Bielefeld: transcript, 2009).

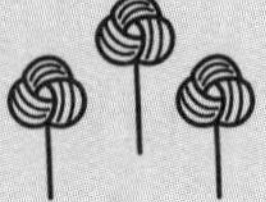

Dirtgold

Orla Barry

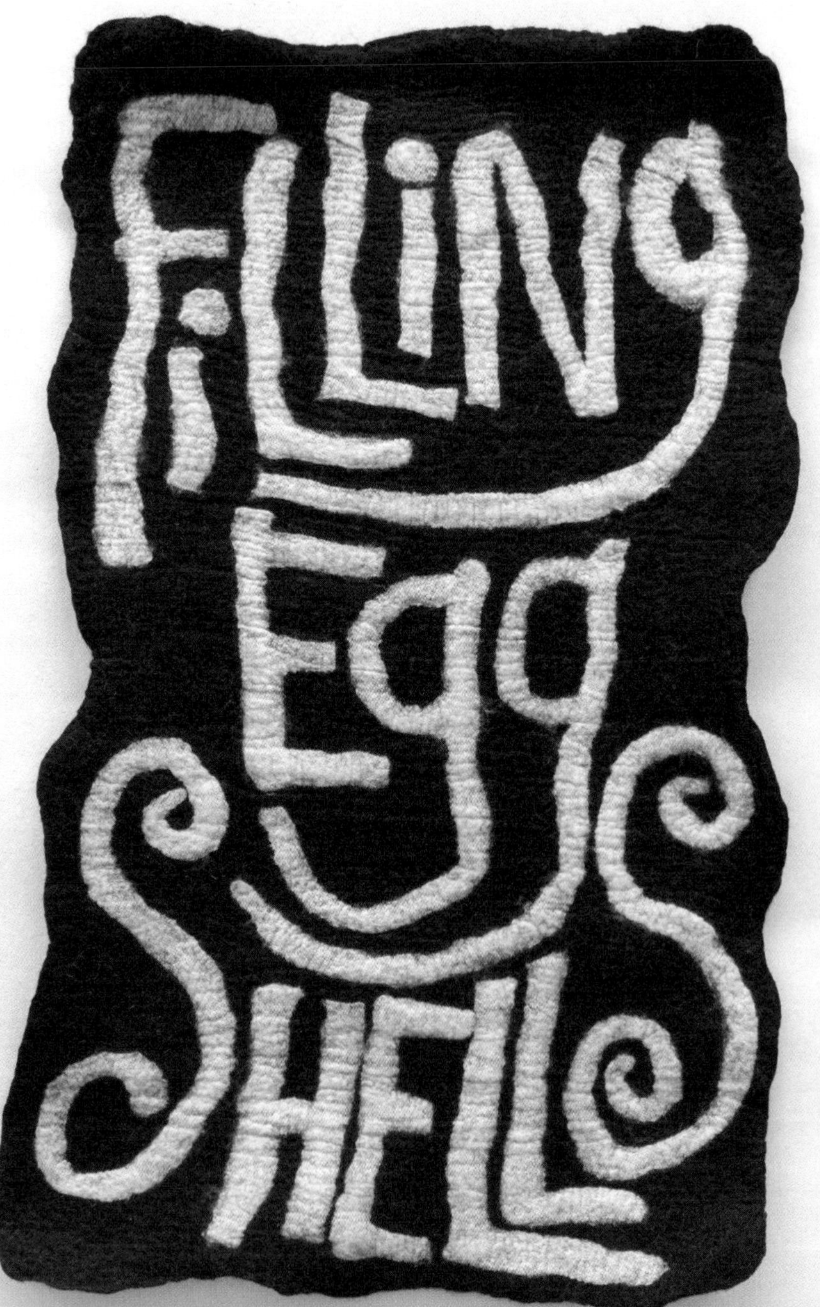
FiLiNG
Egg
SHELLS

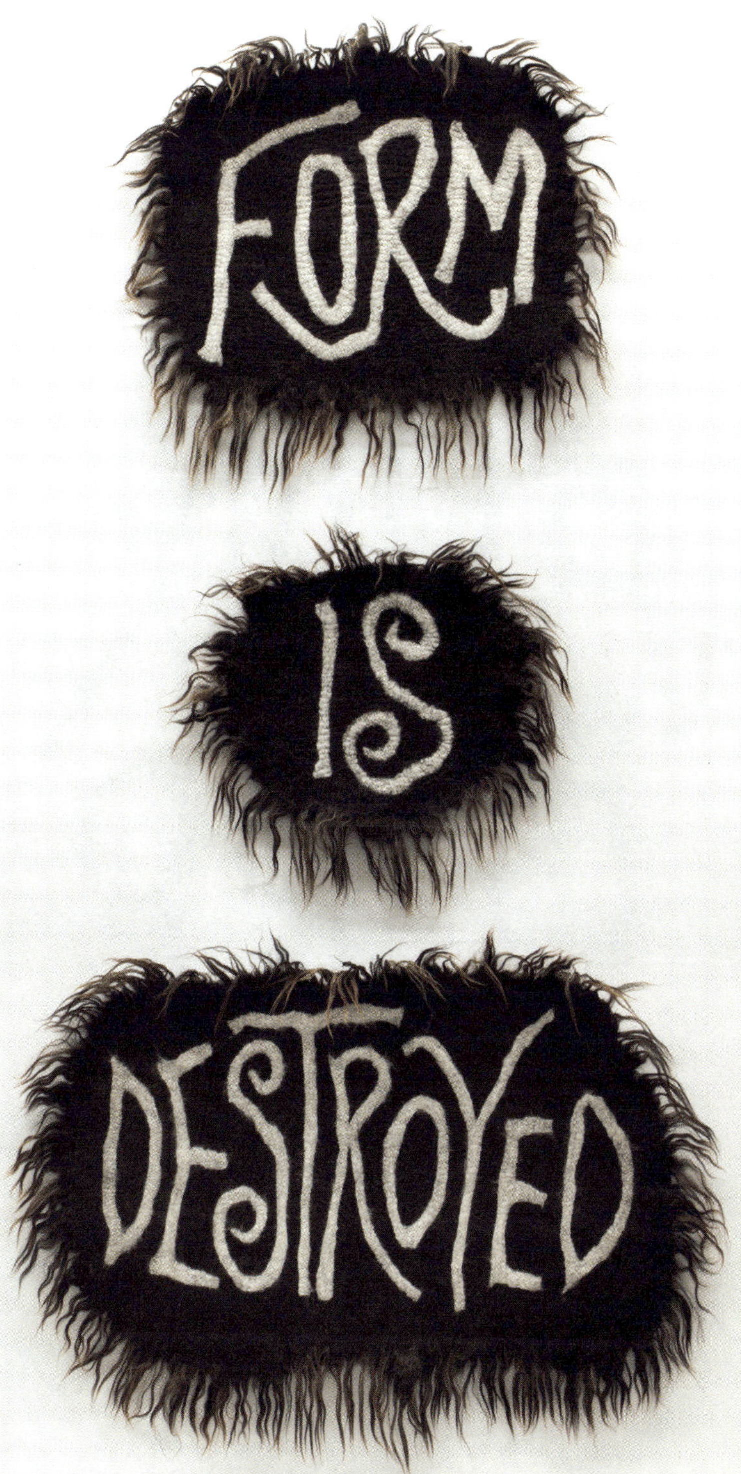
FORM
IS
DESTROYED

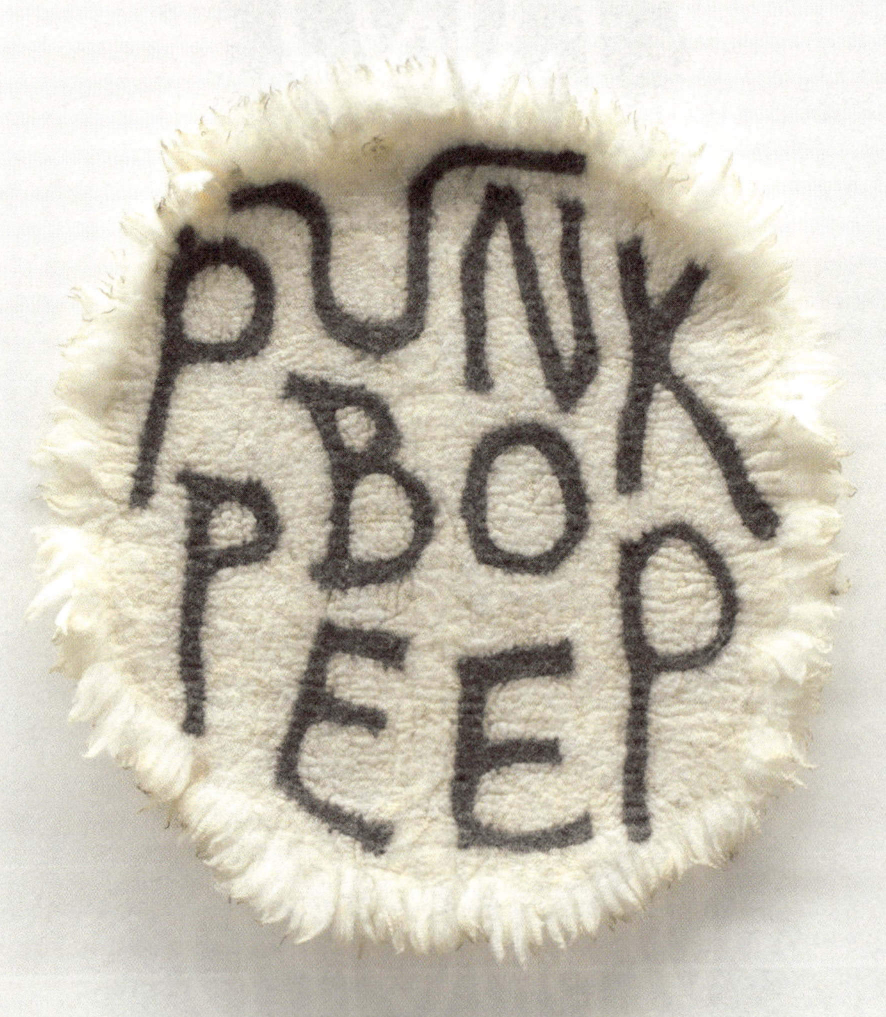
PUNK
BO
PEEP

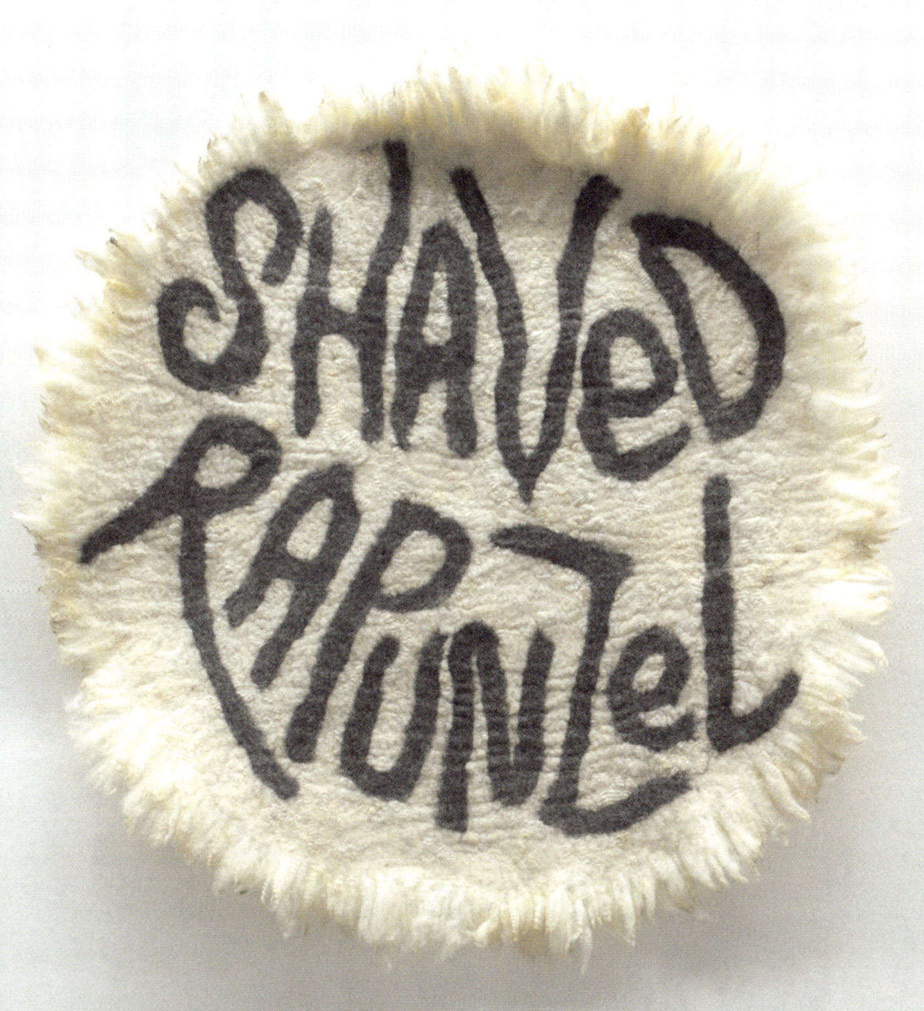
SHAVED
RAPUNZEL

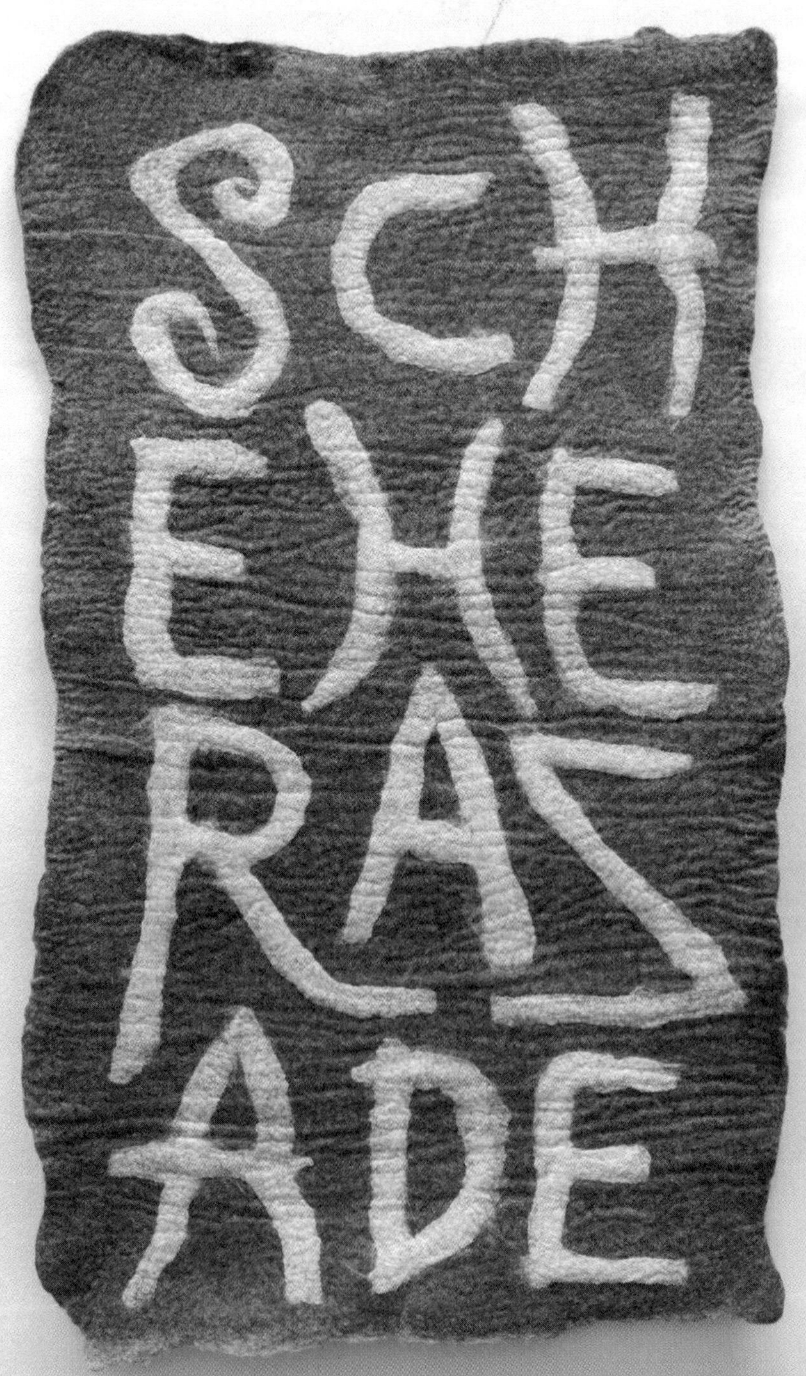
SCH
EHE
RAZ
ADE

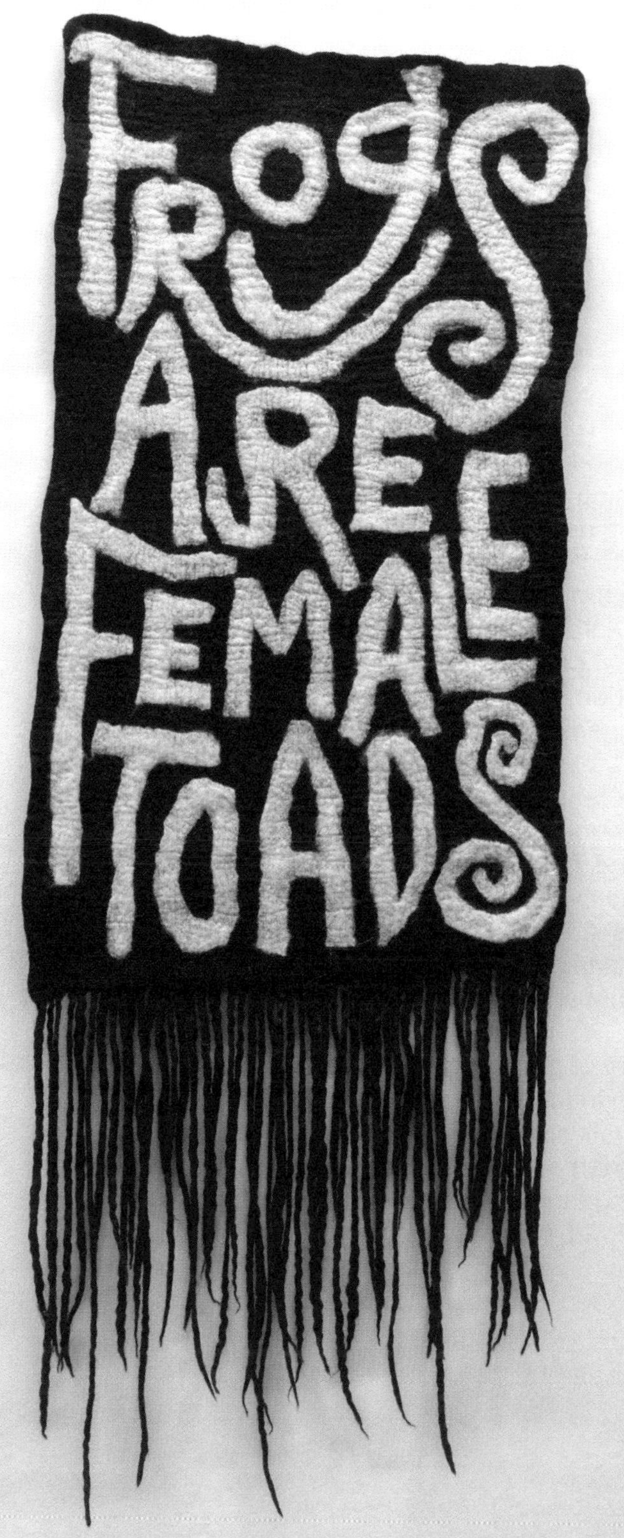
FROGS
ARE
FEMALE
TOADS

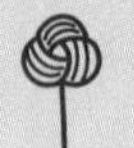

There is something ecopolitical for me about making these felt works from scratch. The physical labor and the work of times past. The repetitive gestures of shearing, washing, carding, and felting raw wool from my own sheep and other peoples' sheep with my own hands.

Creating value where there is none. Creating value through time spent. Giving wool a voice: speaking in dark, dystopian tones.

The felt works are directly inspired by the farm and the animals I am collaborating with and learning from. It has been a long road—fourteen years long now. From farming to felting to genetics and livestock showing: a perennial labor of love, adopting the past to understand the future. An ongoing autoethnographic-artistic study.

I can make psychological artifacts from wool, but am I doing this to draw attention to the material itself? A rhetorical gesture? Or am I a blind and terrified guide?

Sheep were bred and genetically selected for their wool; that's why they look like they do. Wool, a beautiful, highly valued material has become a worthless by-product. My own wool from 2020 and 2021 was stored and exhibited as an artwork in 2022 because its value would not even cover the work of the shearer.

It's the real metaphorical pile. The material poetry of our dying world. Can the family farm survive in Ireland? Can nature survive with it? How can city folk support farmers directly? How can farmers with a creative voice influence the industry? Can young farmers do things differently? Work in harmony with nature? Give something back and still survive? Keep it smallish and ethical and still survive? Keep it ecological and still survive? Look how farmers are struggling. What a moral dilemma we are all in. And how it all matters now...

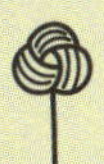

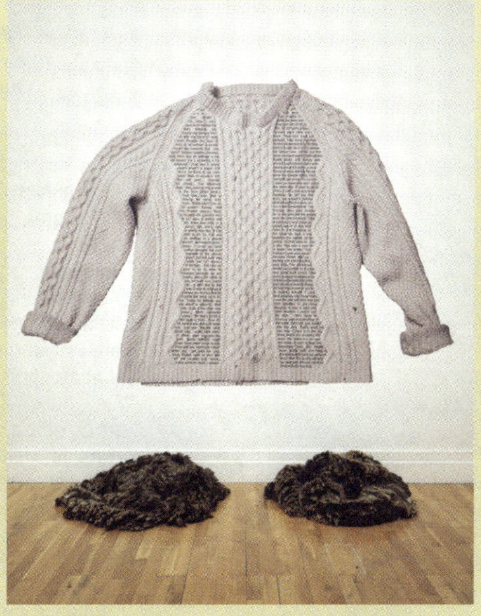

p. 130
Filling Egg Shells, felted raw wool from Hebridean, Tiroler Bergschaf and Merino sheep, 140 × 85 cm, 2023

p. 131
Form Is Destroyed, felted raw wool from Tiroler Bergschaf, Lleyn, Merino and Drenthe Heath sheep, 106 × 85 cm, 2024

p. 132
Punk Bo-Peep, felted raw wool from Gotland and Merino sheep, 107 × 107 cm, 2023

p. 133
Shaved Rapunzel, felted raw wool from Tiroler Bergschaf, Lleyn and Gotland sheep, 110 × 100 cm, 2024

p. 134
Sheherazade, felted raw wool from Gotland and Merino sheep, 150 × 85 cm, 2023

p. 135
Frogs Are Female Toads, felted raw wool from Hebridean, Tiroler Bergschaf and Merino sheep,200 × 80 cm, 2023

p. 137
The Wool Merchant's Calculator & The Curator's Jumper, 200 × 300 cm, 2022
Exhibition view, A Growing Enquiry—Art & Agriculture, Reconciling Values, RHA Gallery, Dublin, 2022

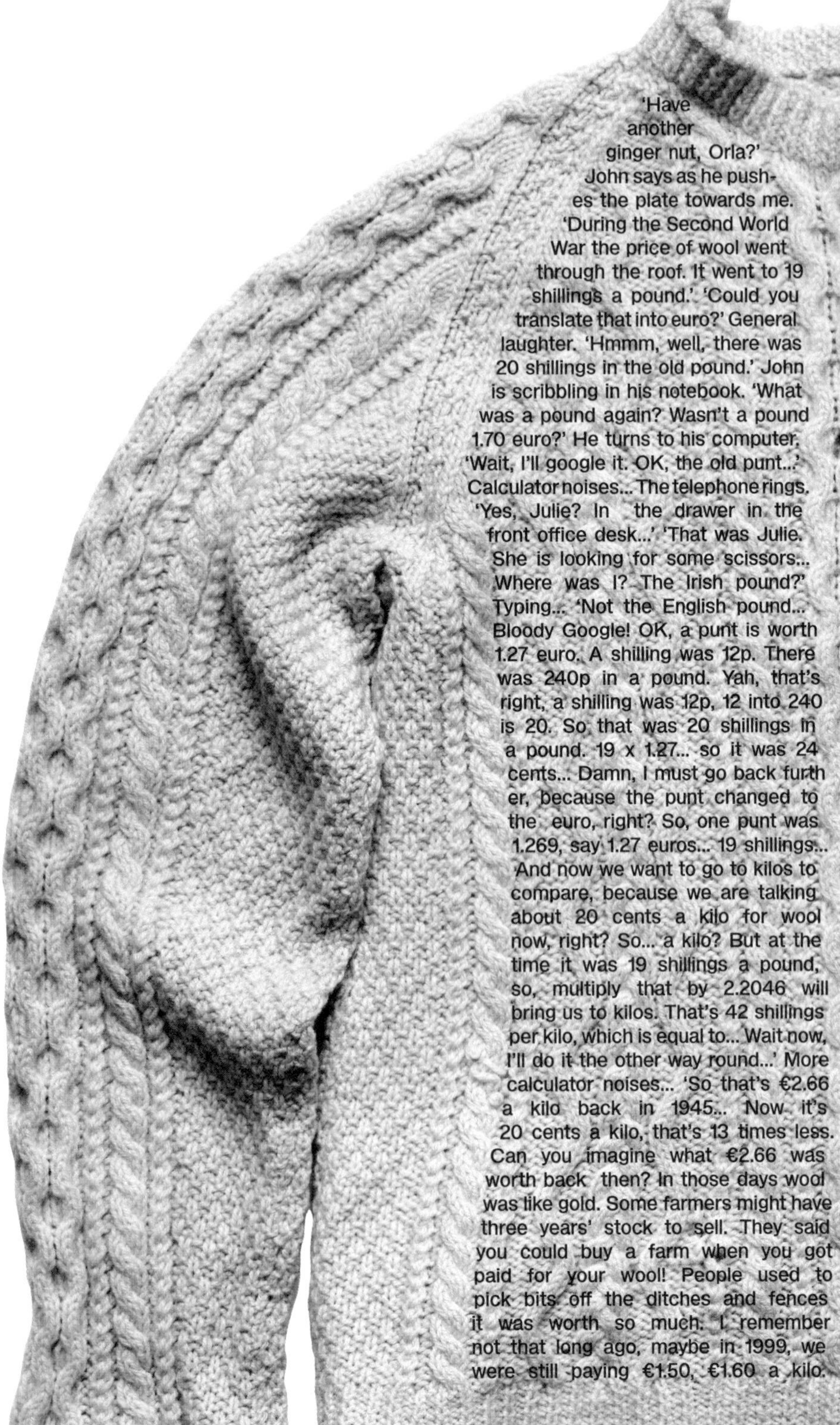

'Have another ginger nut, Orla?' John says as he pushes the plate towards me. 'During the Second World War the price of wool went through the roof. It went to 19 shillings a pound.' 'Could you translate that into euro?' General laughter. 'Hmmm, well, there was 20 shillings in the old pound.' John is scribbling in his notebook. 'What was a pound again? Wasn't a pound 1.70 euro?' He turns to his computer. 'Wait, I'll google it. OK, the old punt...' Calculator noises... The telephone rings. 'Yes, Julie? In the drawer in the front office desk...' 'That was Julie. She is looking for some scissors... Where was I? The Irish pound?' Typing... 'Not the English pound... Bloody Google! OK, a punt is worth 1.27 euro. A shilling was 12p. There was 240p in a pound. Yah, that's right, a shilling was 12p, 12 into 240 is 20. So that was 20 shillings in a pound. 19 x 1.27... so it was 24 cents... Damn, I must go back further, because the punt changed to the euro, right? So, one punt was 1.269, say 1.27 euros... 19 shillings... And now we want to go to kilos to compare, because we are talking about 20 cents a kilo for wool now, right? So... a kilo? But at the time it was 19 shillings a pound, so, multiply that by 2.2046 will bring us to kilos. That's 42 shillings per kilo, which is equal to... Wait now, I'll do it the other way round...' More calculator noises... 'So that's €2.66 a kilo back in 1945... Now it's 20 cents a kilo, that's 13 times less. Can you imagine what €2.66 was worth back then? In those days wool was like gold. Some farmers might have three years' stock to sell. They said you could buy a farm when you got paid for your wool! People used to pick bits off the ditches and fences it was worth so much. I remember not that long ago, maybe in 1999, we were still paying €1.50, €1.60 a kilo.

At 20 cents a kilo, farmers don't care anymore. They just give you garbage. They bring the wool up here all wet and dirty. All they want is to get rid of it. It's always the farmer who comes out the worst. He has to pay €2.50 to get the sheep shorn, and there's only about 2.2 kg in a fleece. So, you're talking about 50 cents for your fleece of wool, and the farmer gives the shearer €2.50. He's losing €2 per sheep. It's a mess. I gave up exporting wool about five years ago. It used to go to China. I had a few very good contacts. To tell you the truth, we couldn't believe what we got for the wool. Jesus, it was like gold dust. The Chinese were mad looking for it. We sent out the greasy wool. We sold lorryloads. They processed it and made jumpers out of it and sold them to the Russians! In the good old days, I was doubling my money. I'd be selling 20,000 kilos at 1.50 a kilo profit. That was a nice little touch.' He smiles. 'The transport was also cheap because China was exporting a lot and importing very little. The containers would be coming to Europe and going back empty. They were so happy to get anything in them at all. I was able to export a load of wool to China for less than a load of spuds to Galway. Actually, I once sold potatoes into Hong Kong. I was the only one who ever sold Irish potatoes to the Hongkongers. It was a total and utter disaster; I nearly lost my shirt... We'll have to finish up here, that lorryload of flat-pack furniture just pulled into the yard. That's what I'm into now. I store it in the big shed where you dropped the wool.' He takes me to see the place. It used to look like something from the Middle Ages, dusty, dark, and filled to the ceiling with bursting sacks of wool. Now it's all strip lighting, as neat and efficient as Ikea. I feel an ovine teardrop.

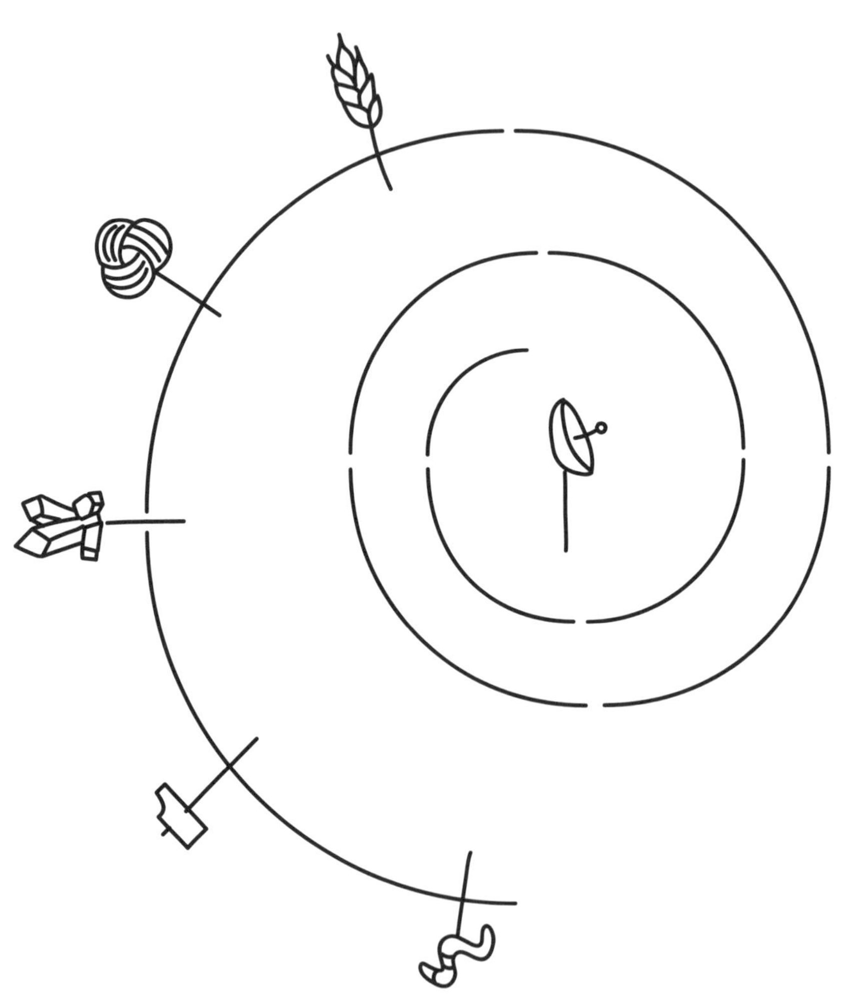

When the Sun Sets East

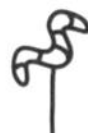

Kateryna Aliinyk

In anatomy illustrations from the seventeenth century, the human figure—parts of it without skin or muscle—is depicted against a background of nature. Some of the figures lean against tree trunks or bare their dismembered legs upon moss-covered stones. With one hand, it exposes its abdominal cavity, while also managing to gently touch a lily growing nearby with the other hand. The person in the picture holds the lily and their flesh with equal ease, with just two fingers. The combination of the dismembered yet perfectly alive figure and the burgeoning weeds and branches is striking, and the windflaw pictured in some of the illustrations is sure to carry small insects and dust particles, which in such conditions will inevitably end up adhering to the bare meat.

With each subsequent illustration, the figure gradually peels off layer after layer, while still managing to interact with the nature around it. By the changing flora, you would think it is also taking a walk in the process. As it makes its way along, it removes almost every part of its body until only the legs remain, revealing to our eyes the peaceful landscape hiding behind the figure. Even without a torso, the legs continue to stand on the ground with the same confidence and ease.

The morphing of the indifferent view of nature toward this act and the tranquility of the figure in those illustrations pierced me like a dagger. There is neither pain nor pity in it, nor, even more so, sadness.

Obviously the illustrations carry a very different practical meaning, but with the outbreak of war, such mundanity of vulnerability and horror combined with sensitivity slammed both into my native landscape and into me every time I visited. Of course, without visible manifestation, because the very topography of these places for me has been slowly moving from physical space to sensual-cognitive space for some time now.

Now in my dreams, fantasies, and memories, when I visit my native land, I see that everything there has also ripened and burst. Horror is very multicolored indeed, and because it has been here for so long and has touched so many things, the relationship with it has also become different: complex and profound. Next to the fear, there is serenity and tenderness and an even more steadfast, almost neurotic attention to details that smash the dense solid background of such immense events as war into undertones. Now, you can reach many things with your eyes alone, yet the distance is also very beautiful and fruitful.

During one such journey in my dreams, my mother and I are walking toward the end of our vegetable patch in Sloviansk, and we see the following picture: someone has brought a bunch of equipment to dismantle Mount Karachun, cutting off piece after piece. One side of it is almost gone, and we are just standing there and watching. Mother is crying: "What're we going to do without the mountain? It'll be so empty, just fields!" "What is its value anyway?" my grandmother says. "So they'll dismantle it. Let it go."

Although Karachun looks more like a long hill, the experience of it, like that of any other mountain, is solid and unshakable, just how the relationship with the native landscape feels, as opposed to the relationships with people. You do not even expect such a surprise as an abrupt loss of connection. The contemplation of nature and the presence of war are perhaps the two most vivid and sensual experiences of my life. The variations of their interconnectedness are endless.

Nature gives me a sense of density that is hard to penetrate, and looking at it from afar I feel particularly tempted to find a way to do so.

Looking out the car window on my short trips to the East, I imagined myself cutting the body of the landscape with a knife. I cut, as if it was a cake, a slice of everything the eye can grasp—sky, flora, fauna—and ate it. If I had known those trips were the last ones, I would have tried to touch everything to the fullest—with my eyes, mouth, hands—to memorize it better.

In my fantasies, I gracefully and effortlessly, as if it were a shirt, pull up the skin on my torso, just like those figures in the illustrations, and rest my meat against that very landscape. And of course, just as I imagined, the gravel, dirt, and dust stick to me, but that's okay, I'm just dreaming. Then I draw down the skin, and it adheres instantly, without complication, so that inside, on another layer of me, there will be another part of the landscape, along with the one I ate. It is almost like wanting to taste a mud cake as a child, but the scale of desire is different, matching the grandeur of events in those lands.

Consequently, the way my native rural landscape fed my body is not even closely comparable to the way it fed my imagination. Hidden in almost everything I do today in art is a love letter to the landscape, a love letter to the fruit, the insects, and the soil. Only with a brushstroke or a word can I touch those places now, caress them, and thank them for everything.

With a distorted perception it is not easy to assess what space I actually occupied, and most importantly how much space it was. The most visible form of presence was probably my work in the three vegetable gardens of my childhood, where neither the process nor the result interested me at the time. It was not about indifference or disappointment, but the apple, for example, turned out to be wormy, as always. What was wrong with it?

Grandmother: "This apple is indeed very good, you can't throw it away. A worm always knows which apple is better than the others."

"Great! Next time I find a wormy apple, I'll make sure to be pleased and eat the part the worm left for me."

Raspberry, on the other hand, smells like stinky bugs, and homegrown bell pepper is bitter, with a hard, thick peel. Bugs on all berries, maggots in cherries, which means: everything is organic? And the best. It still tastes bad and unpleasant, but I understand Grandma: love makes you turn a blind eye to many things. But I found the smell of rotten cherries very good—better than that of the fresh ones—they had a more cherry-like smell. It was so tantalizing that I thought all the artificial fruit and berry smells in candy were synthesized from rotten or almost overripened fruit. Smelling and looking is very mind-whirring—something completely different from eating—because when the smell was better than the taste, I felt I had been cheated.

Now I realize that my conditions were not perfect enough to fall in love with the practical aspects of a rural landscape, but I made attempts. At home there was a lot of talk about the qualities of different flavors, especially the value and healthiness of bitterness, which made me develop my own approach to consumption: "If I eat only fruit, my body runs the risk of becoming too shiny—sweet but sickly. If I eat only vegetables, on the other hand, I run the risk of not being passionate enough. When I eat vegetables, I think about the health of my body. When I eat fruit, I think about eroticism. At home we grow mostly vegetables. I hardly ever eat fruit."

And this is just one of the beautiful paradoxes that made up life in the countryside.

In my memory of the summer of 2014, I was fifteen years old. The war had just started, but I still couldn't wrap my head around it. It delaminated with the dreams and fantasies of that young and tender age, like water and oil, yet at some point they osculated. After another exhausting day of work in the garden, I looked into the distance. The sky was so red, as if the fate of mankind was being decided beyond the mountain. Suddenly I felt the need to look back at the most dramatic things in my life, to live this moment to the fullest, at least to pay respects to such a background, but nothing immediately came to mind. So I decided to run across the field under this bloody sky, like a protagonist from classic literature. And my skirt, by all means, had to cling to the tall weeds. After all, there's a reason Flaubert focused so much on the costume description paired with an event. From the books, I then concluded that the completeness and success of an even simplistic drama were based on well-selected details and gestures.

I walked toward the end of the garden and ran through the field. Grasshoppers started jumping out of the bushes, catching on my skirt, going straight into my mouth, which was open due to overexcitement. As I continued to run, I kept it open so they could jump out. They were luckier than the ones I squeezed in my flip-flops. Since that summer, the word "juicy" has unfortunately become forever associated with crushed insects.

It is clear why exactly such nonsensical but real details are absent from my favorite books; they make the drama ridiculous rather than sublime. And it was just as ridiculous and naive to see the landscape as merely a backdrop for my experiences and adventures.

On my way home, I thought I always wanted to be the kind person who would never step on a bug, much less destroy dozens of them for the sake of a silly storyline.

"Tomorrow I will bring home pockets full of snails because they like to eat grapes, while ants like sugar and citric acid."

Later, a fly came to live in my room, and for the first time, I was not only happy about it, I even thought I had grown to love it. One evening, as usual, but this time especially insistently, it wanted to sit on my head—and then it disappeared. I did not know how long flies live, but the window was closed the whole time.

Immediately after the fly disappeared, I suddenly felt more compassion than ever toward my great-grandmother's dog. After all, sometimes they fed him only with beets and potato peels. Dogs in the village often have a difficult life as they produce neither milk, meat, nor eggs. They are at the bottom of the backyard hierarchy, and nobody even cleans up their shit in a timely manner. They run, spreading it with a heavy chain around their kennel.

Soon, even the sight of the oozing guts of those very beets, accidentally cut with a shovel, brought tears to my eyes. Everything seemed so alive and spirited, so unbearably sorry I was for everything. “Is it possible that if you have ever in your life seen, really looked closely at these things, you will want to destroy something? I wish every field mouse here would die of old age!” In such revelations, I stayed there for a couple of months, and soon we left those lands indefinitely.

Love during war is as multicolored as horror—so sharp and piercing that it penetrates where I do not expect to feel it at all. And then details like the pervasive feeling caused by seeing the above-mentioned anatomy illustrations collide with the memory of grasshoppers crushed in my flip-flops.

Obviously, my presence has not improved or fertilized those lands in any beautiful way, and feelings about everything are now so easy to diminish or exaggerate. But I really think we have a special relationship. My landscape and I parted ways ten years ago, and from afar, it is as clear as can be that it was not just a backway if my absence is just my own personal tragedy; it’s not like the grass has stopped being green or the sky has stopped being blue. Maybe it seems even more blue against the dark earth of long-untouched fields.

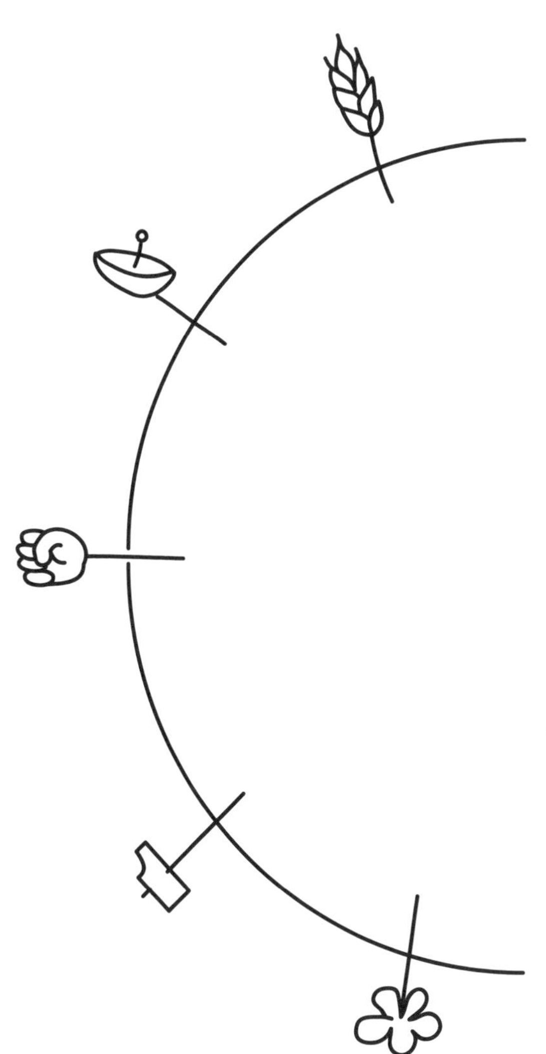

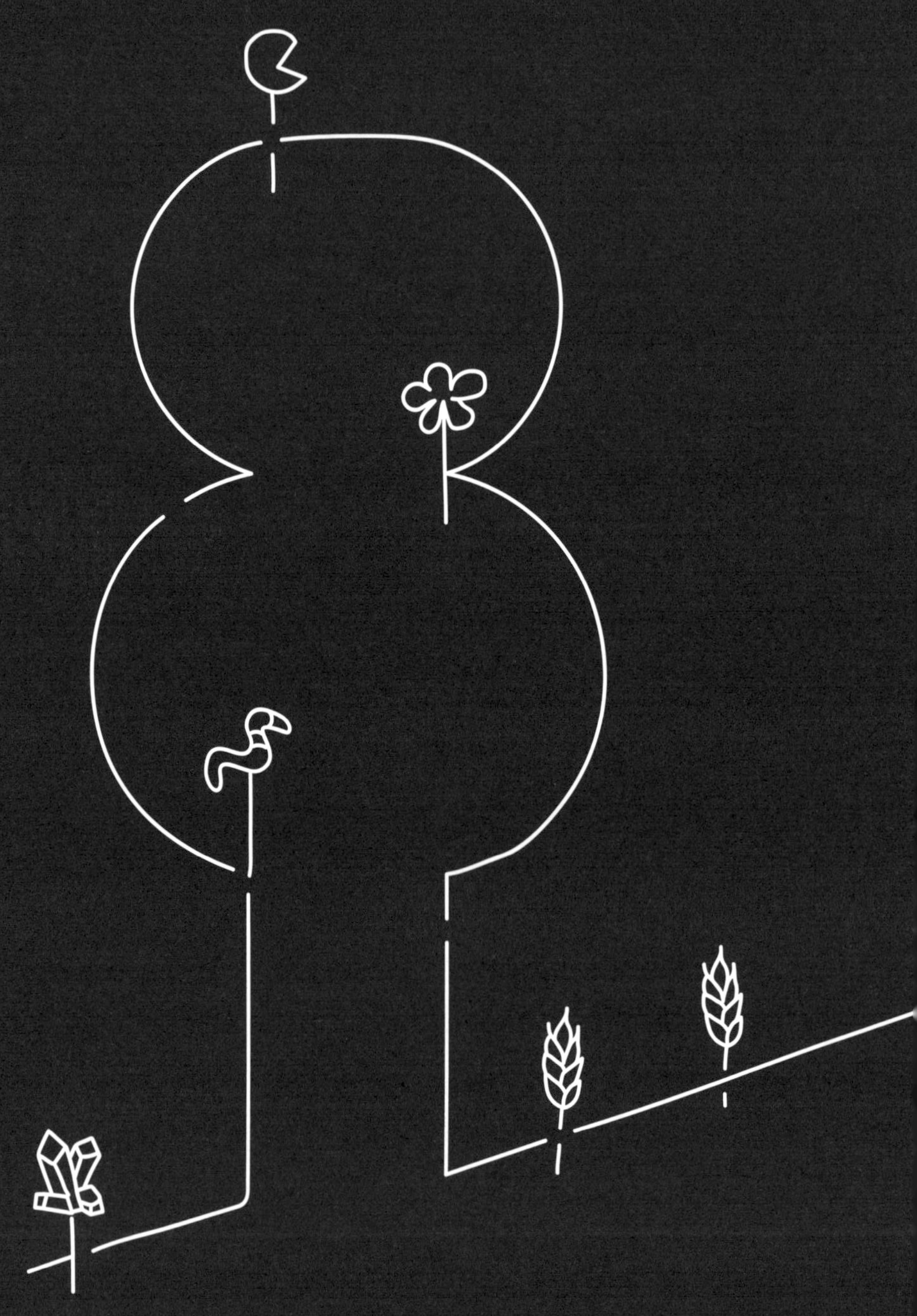

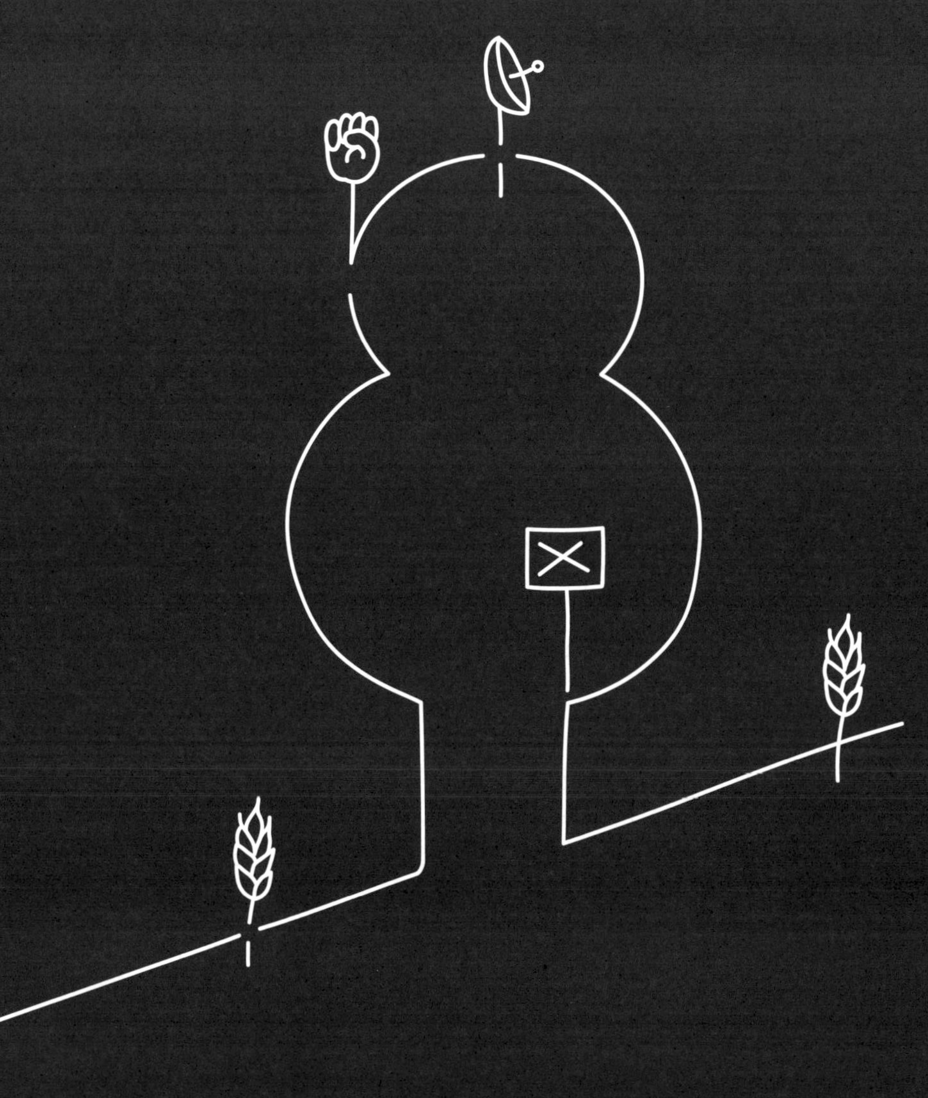

Glossary
of Symbols

Aleksei Borisionok, Katalin Erdődi, The Rodina

Book Reading books helps transfer knowledge from generation to generation, from struggle to struggle. But we must keep in mind: not all forms of knowledge or stories enter into books; some of them are passed on orally.

Cereal Crops During the second half of the 20th century, there was a significant increase in the production of cereal crops worldwide, which made cereals the world's largest crops. They therefore represent the world of the rural and the countryside.

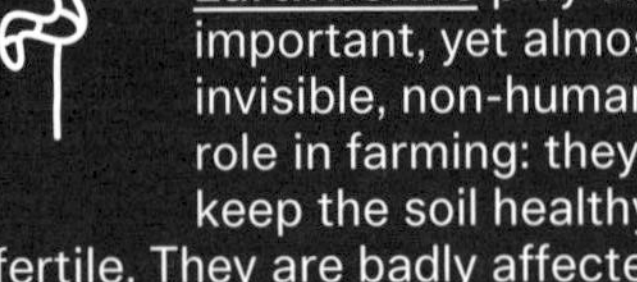

Earthworms play an important, yet almost invisible, non-human role in farming: they keep the soil healthy and fertile. They are badly affected by the synthetic chemicals used in industrial agriculture. For organic farmers, their presence is especially important: earthworms are proof that they work the land in an ecological way. In this sense, these creatures are symbols of agroecological change.

Flower For many of us, flowers are part of our everyday lives. They are symbols of beauty and a good life, but also the passing of time. Certain flowers have been used as symbols in political movements, like the women's movement ("Bread and Roses") and socialism (red carnation). Even revolutions are named after flowers (the Rose Revolution in Georgia).

Gear A gear is a rotating circular machine part with cut teeth. It is used in various machines and devices. A gear is also a well-known symbol of various workers movements and trade unions because it symbolizes how workers support each other.

A **Hammer** is probably the most common tool of workers. The hammer is also used as a political symbol in many trade unions as well as workers' and communist movements.

The **Harvest** has been an important topic in the history of art. Some artists show the hard work, others the freshly picked crops or the celebrations. A good harvest means the community will not experience hunger; it is a symbol of good life.

Haystacks are common features of rural landscapes and part of our imaginaries of the rural, especially within a European context. They demonstrate the diversity of the countryside: the ways in which they are stacked vary according to different cultures and geographies, but also through time and modernization. Artists often document haystacks in landscape painting and photography, but they also use them in more experimental ways, for performative actions such as the legendary action-installation *Hay-Straw* by Zorka Ságlová.

A **Mineral** is a solid substance that results from many thousands of years of geologic processes in the ground. Minerals are used by everyone—we have them in simple metal items as well as in modern high-tech devices. For example, one smartphone contains more than forty different minerals. At the same time, minerals can challenge our rational systems of thinking such as science. They can be used in spellcasting, magic, and rituals.

Pac-Man / Pie Chart Pac-Man is a computer game in which the player must eat all the dots inside a maze and avoid ghosts. It looks like an open mouth and is often connected with greediness because it eats everything up. Pie charts look similar to Pac-Man due to their circular shape. Divided into slices, they show proportions, for example: of all the people in the Czech Republic, how many buy their food in supermarkets and how many grow it themselves?

Pill We take pills to treat sicknesses and improve physical or mental health. The spread of pills is connected to the global medical-industrial complex, in which some pills cost a fortune, and some basic pills are not even available. Health crises such as the global pandemics of HIV/AIDS or the recent coronavirus make social and economic tensions in society more visible.

Protest Sign The tools we use to protest can be very different: some people make signs and banners, others use their everyday work tools, while yet others light or spit fire.

The **Raised Fist**, or the clenched fist, is a symbol of solidarity, especially within a political movement. It is used in many left-wing movements, especially socialism, anarchism, and trade unionism.

The **Rake**, especially the landscaping rake, is used to shape the landscape, to smooth and grade large patches of earth. Parks and other green areas require a lot of work from gardeners. This is also true for the Lidice Memorial site: there is constant care for the landscape. Earlier, this work of care and maintenance was done by the "Lidice women," the survivors who returned to the village after the war.

Roots It is through their roots that plants absorb and store the nourishment they need from the soil. Similarly, one could say our origins form the basis for our identity, symbolizing our attachment to a certain place, land, or culture.

Satellites are used for communication, broadcasting, navigation, but also weather forecasting and Earth observation. In this sense, they are our daily messengers of climate change. They help us understand the critical situation we are in and enable us to think about the future.

The **Scythe** is a basic tool of farmers, symbolizing both manual labor and resistance to industrialization. Its curved blade offers an alternative to mechanized harvesters, embodying grassroots empowerment and the resilience of rural communities. Straightened scythes and pitchforks have been used as a weapon in peasant uprisings by those who did not have access to more expensive weapons.

The **Shovel** is an instrument of patience and endurance, symbolizing exhaustive manual work. It is utilized by mining workers, soldiers digging trenches, and archaeologists unearthing artifacts of the past. Extracting fossils from the ground and unearthing archaeological objects often rely on the same principles of colonial domination.

A **Sickle** can be used for grafting, cutting and other ways to take care of the crops. It has been an important symbol in peasant movements. Together with a hammer, it represented a political alliance between the industrial working class and the peasantry, often misused and betrayed by the ruling class of socialist states.

Water Irrigation The construction of watering systems like canals has been key to the expansion of industrial agriculture because it enables the production of more crops. At the same time, more intensive irrigation and the bad management of water resources can cause irreparable damage to local ecosystems.

Wind Turbines convert the kinetic energy of the wind into electric energy. Today they play an important part in the "green transition," the change to more sustainable energy alternatives like wind or solar power. Therefore more and more wind turbines are built in the countryside. This often leads to conflict: not everybody is happy about how they are changing rural landscapes.

Wool Humans have been washing, weaving and wearing wool since ancient times. Wool used to be very valuable. It was an important raw material in the textile industry and global trade. Today wool has lost much of its value and sheep farmers have difficulties selling it.

The symbols created by The Rodina for the visual identity of the Biennale Matter of Art introduce various tools, notions, gestures, living beings and materials that make up the complex political landscapes the curators and invited contributors are navigating. These tools can serve the dominant political regime, or they can also be used against their masters. The glossary also served as a mediation tool in the exhibition.

Kateryna Aliinyk
Kyiv, * Luhansk, Ukraine, 1998
In 2016 Kateryna Aliinyk moved to Kyiv, where she entered the National Academy of Fine Arts and Architecture, receiving a master's degree in painting in 2021. In 2020 she completed a contemporary art course at KAMA (Kyiv Academy of Media Art) and the program Positions of the Artist offered by Method Fund. Her main media are painting and text, and she works mostly with the topic of the landscape touched by the war and occupation in Donbas. She works through images of nature and non-anthropocentric optics.

I Feel You, group exhibition, PinchukArtCentre, Kyiv, Ukraine, 2024
Kyiv Biennial 2023, tranzit.at, Vienna, Austria, 2023
Motherland, group exhibition, Museum Ephraim-Palais, Berlin, Germany, 2023
40th EVA International – Ireland's Biennial of Contemporary Art, Limerick, Ireland, 2023
How do we turn Salt into Sugar?, group exhibition, Galerie ETAGE in Museum Reinickendorf, Berlin, Germany, 2023

Orla Barry
Duncormick, * Wexford, Ireland, 1969
Orla Barry is both a visual artist and a shepherd. She lives and works on the south coast of Ireland, where she runs a successful flock of pedigree Lleyn sheep flock alongside her art practice. Barry writes as well as makes performances and video and sound installations. Her work focuses on language, both written and spoken, as well as its visual deconstruction and displacement. Fiction, autoethnography, and oral history are blended to reflect on the culture of our disconnection from the countryside and the boundaries of art and the rural everyday. Barry plays with the fractured relationship between agriculture, gender, and the natural world. Her work also deals with the materiality of words and approaches to writing and speaking to accentuatinge this physical and embodied understanding of language as visual form.

Shaved Rapunzel & La Petite Bergère Punk, Musée des Arts Contemporains au Grand-Hornu, Boussu, Belgium, 2024
40th EVA International – Ireland's Biennial of Contemporary Art, Limerick, Ireland, 2023
Spin Spin Scheherazade, performance and exhibition, Dublin Theatre Festival, Temple Bar Gallery, Dublin, Ireland; Midsummer Festival, Crawford Art Gallery, Cork, Ireland; Wexford Arts Center, Wexford, Ireland; Playground Festival, M Leuven, Leuven, Belgium; Kaaistudios, Brussels, Belgium; Mu.ZEE, Ostend, Belgium, 2019–2023
A Growing Enquiry – Art & Agriculture, Reconciling Values, RHA Gallery, Dublin, Ireland, 2022
Wintrum Frod (with Els Dietvorst), Mu.ZEE, Ostend, Belgium, 2019

Aleksei Borisionok
Vienna, * Minsk, Belarus, 1992
Aleksei Borisionok is a curator, writer, and organizer who currently lives and works in Vienna. He is a member of the artistic-research group Problem Collective and the Work Hard! Play Hard! working group. He writes about art and politics for various magazines, catalogs, and online platforms such as *e-flux Journal*, *L'Internationale Online*, *Partisan*, *Springerin*, and *Paletten*, among many others. He was a fellow at the Vera List Center in New York (2022–2024).

Borisionok, Aleksei. "Queer Temporalities and Protest Infrastructures in Belarus, 2020–22: A Brief Museum Guide." *e-flux Journal*, no. 127 (May 2022): 85–95.

Borisionok, Aleksei and Olia Sosnovskaya. "The Futures of the 'East'". In *Baltic Triennial 14: The Endless Frontier (A Reader)*, edited by Valentinas Klimašauskas and João Laia. Vilnius: Contemporary Art Centre (CAC); Milan: Mousse Publishing, 2022.

Borisionok, Aleksei. "The Secret Museum of the Workers Movement." In "Towards a Weak Realism." *Lulu-journal*, no. 9 (February 2021).

If Disrupted, it Becomes Tangible, exhibition curated by Aleksei Borisionok and Antonina Stebur,, National Art Gallery, Vilnius, Lithuania, 2023

Every Day. Art, Solidarity, Resistance, exhibition curated by Aleksei Borisionok, Andrei Dureika, Marina Naprushkina, Sergey Shabohin, Antonina Stebur, and Maxim Tyminko,, Mystetskyi Arsenal, Kyiv, Ukraine, 2021

Ramona Duminicioiu

Ionești, * Drăgășani, Romania, 1983

Ramona Duminicioiu is the president of the Eco Ruralis association, which represents the interests of peasants at the national level. She is part of the coordination committee of the Ukrainian Rural Development Network (URDN). She is involved in the coordination of a regional alliance for the development of agroecology and the implementation of peasants' rights in Eastern Europe and Central Asia (BILIM). From 2016 to 2020 she was part of the coordination committee of the peasant confederation Via Campesina Europa (ECVC). From 2017 to 2021 she was part of the coordination committee of the Civil Society and Indigenous Peoples' Mechanism for Relations with the UN Committee on World Food Security (CSIPM-CFS). In 2018 she played the role of an expert in the final negotiation session of the UN Declaration on the Rights of Peasants and Other People Working in Rural Areas (UNDROP), which was adopted that same year by the Human Rights Council in Geneva and later by the UN General Assembly in New York. In her household in Ionești, Duminicioiu cultivates grapes, corn, and other vegetables with her extended family.

Duminicioiu, Ramona, ed. "Manual on the implementation of the UN Declaration for the Rights of Peasants and Other People Working in Rural Areas (UNDROP) in Eastern Europe and Central Asia: A tool designed for Governments, public servants, peasants and small scale family farmers associations, international organizations, donors, civil society at large and academic institutions." FAO Europe and Central Asia and Eco Ruralis – Romanian Peasants Association. Accessed May 17, 2023. http://www.undrop-implementation.info.

Duminicioiu, Ramona. "Whoever Does Not Have Peasants, Should Find Them: The Food Injustice of Pandemics." *Undisciplined Environments*, April 9, 2020. https://undisciplinedenvironments.org/2020/04/09/whoever-does-not-have-peasants-should-find-them-the-food-injustice-of-pandemics/.

Duminicioiu, Ramona, "Drepturile Țăranilor și Agroecologia în România" [Peasants rights and agroecology in Romania]. Eco Ruralis – Romanian Peasants Association. Accessed May 17, 2024. https://www.ecoruralis.ro/2023/08/07/taranii-polenizatorii-si-agroecologia/

eeefff

Minsk/Berlin

eeefff is an artistic cooperation / made-up institution / cybernetic political brigade / poetic computations / hacking unit / queer time. it is not any one of these, nor all together. active since 2013. eeefff makes software-based projects, publications, networks, and platforms that critically explore digital labor, value extraction, and community formation. methods include: public actions, online interventions, performative seminars, software and hardware hacking, framing environments and choreographing social situations.

eeefff.org

Katalin Erdődi

Vienna/Budapest, * Debrecen, Hungary, 1980

Katalin Erdődi is a curator, dramaturg, and writer. Her cross-disciplinary practice spans socially engaged art, experimental performance, and site-specific collaborations in rural and urban public space. Her recent curatorial research focuses on critical rural art practices and investigates social change in rural areas through collaborative approaches that involve people from very different backgrounds in the artistic process. She is especially interested in the post-socialist transformations of Central and Eastern Europe, which she strives to address with decolonizing, feminist methodologies. In 2020 Erdődi received the Igor Zabel Award Grant for her locally embedded and inclusive curatorial practice. She is co-curator of the 2024 edition of the Biennale Matter of Art in Prague as well as a two-year artistic research project *SALT. CLAY. ROCK.* (nGbK Berlin, 2023–2024). From 2025, she will be the new director of Trafó House of Contemporary Arts in Budapest.

Erdődi, Katalin. "Land der Lieder: Agonistische Öffentlickeiten und ländlicher Wandel" [Land of songs: Agonistic public spheres and rural change]. In *Porös-werden: Geteilte Räume, urbane Dramaturgien, performatives Kuratieren* [Becoming porous: Shared spaces, urban dramaturgies, performative curating], edited by Barbara Büscher, Elke Krasny, and Lucie Ortmann, 344–365. Vienna: Turia + Kant, 2024.

Erdődi, Katalin, ed. *We Anarchists Do Not Fret Over Moral Maggots*. A publication of the eponymous exhibition by Igor and Ivan Buharov, curated by Katalin Erdődi. Budapest: Petőfi Literary Museum / Kassák Museum, 2023.

Erdődi, Katalin, Boglárka Börcsök, and Andreas Bolm. "The Future Belongs to Ghosts." *Kajet 05: On Easternfuturism*, edited by Petre Mogoș and Laura Naum, 234–247. Bucharest: Dispozitiv Books, 2022.

Erdődi, Katalin, ed. *We Are Not Made of Sugar, We Are from Concrete*. A publication/songbook of the artistic project News Medley by Alicja Rogalska with Katalin Erdődi, Réka Annus, and the Women's Choir of Kartal. Budapest: OFFBiennale/Oncurating, 2021.

Erdődi, Katalin, and Ame Panzh. "Die solidarische Stadt braucht Vorstellungskraft" [A solidary city needs imagination]. In *Die Stadt als Stätte der Solidarität* [The city as a place of solidarity], edited by Niki Kubaczek and Monika Mokre, 159–180. Vienna: transversal texts, 2021.

Fernando García-Dory

Madrid, * Madrid, Spain, 1978

Fernando García-Dory's work engages the relationship between culture and nature as manifested in multiple contexts, from the landscape and the rural to desires and expectations in relation to identity, crisis, utopia, and social change. Interested in the harmonic complexity of biological forms and processes, his work addresses connections and cooperation, from microorganisms to social systems and from traditional art languages to collaborative agroecological projects and actions. He studied fine art and rural sociology and is preparing his PhD on art and agroecology. In 2009 he started the collaborative platform INLAND—Campo Adentro, where he has focused most of his practice up to today.

García-Dory, Fernando, and Lucia Pietroiusti, eds. *Microhabitable*. Cologne: Walther König Verlag, 2023.
García-Dory, Fernando. "This is Not a Cheese – an Inland Approach." In *Microbiopolitics of Milk*, 250. London: Sternberg Press, 2023.
INLAND, "A Village Plan." In *Agropoetics Reader*, 215–219. Berlin: The Institute for Endotic Research Press, 2020.

Tamás Kaszás
Budapest, * Dunaújváros, Hungary, 1976
Tamás Kaszás is an artist who graduated from the Intermedia Department of the Hungarian Academy of Fine Arts, where he is now a teacher. He usually creates complex projects inspired by theoretical research, applying both traditional and new media in his works. By mixing poetic images with useful inventions in his exhibition practice, individual works of art appear mostly as constellations within the larger framework of installations called visual aid constructions. His projects are based on social and ecological issues and spiritual practices. Keywords like collapse and survival, self-sustainability and autonomy, theory vs. practice, folk science, fictional anthropology, and living in nature might give us an idea about his most prevalent topics. He is a member of two artist duos: Randomroutines (with Krisztián Kristóf, since 2003) and Ex-artists' Collective (with Anikó Loránt, 2003–2020).

Savage Intern, solo exhibition, Hungarian National Gallery, Budapest, Hungray, 2023
40th EVA International – Ireland's Biennial of Contemporary Art, Limerick, Ireland, 2023
documenta fifteen, Kassel, Deutschland, 2022
With Heart and Mind, solo exhibition, Trafó, Budapest, Hungary, 2021
Sci Fi Agit Prop, solo exhibition, de Appel, Amsterdam, Netherlands, 2018
Joy of Surviving, solo exhibition, Calouste Gulbenkian Museum, Lisbon, Portugal, 2017
Exercises in Autonomy, featuring Anikó Loránt (ex-artists' collective), exhibition, Muzeum Sztuki, Łodz, Poland, 2016

Kateřina Kolářová
Prague, * České Budějovice, Czechoslovakia, 1976
Kateřina Kolářová teaches at the Faculty of Humanities of Charles University. For several years she has been studying social imaginaries of otherness and social attitudes towards "disability," mechanisms of exclusion, feminism, and queer/LGBT* identities. Her recent work explores the bio-social dimensions of the metabolism, the relationship between human and non-human lives, ecological dimensions of digestion and how we coexist with microorganisms, toxic chemicals, and other "unclean" elements/entities. She is undertaking research into HIV/AIDS and the politics of collective immunity/susceptibility to viral threats. In collaboration with Eva Kot'atková and the Institute of Anxiety, she prepared the podcast *Studio Dysfunction: On the lives of people with "otherness" in a "normal"*

world. She also collaborated with different galleries and co-curated the exhibition *Disabled by Normality* at DOX in 2013. Her forthcoming monograph *Rehabilitative Postsocialism: Disability, Race, Gender, and Sexuality and the Limits of National Belonging* (Michigan University Press, 2024) explores the post-socialist transformation and its effects on so-called minorities and the social imaginaries of civil society.

Kolářová, Kateřina, and Martina Winkler, eds. *Re/imaginations of Disability in State Socialism: Visions, Promises, Frustrations*. New York: Campus Verlag; Chicago: Chicago University Press, 2021.

Kolářová, Kateřina, ed. *Jinakost – postižení – kritika: Společenské konstrukty nezpůsobilosti a hendikepu* [Otherness – disability – criticism: Social constructions of disability and handicaps]. Prague: SLON, 2012.

Kolářová, Kateřina. "Crip Genealogies from the Postsocialist East." In *Crip Genealogies*, edited by M. Chen, A. Kafer, E. Kim, and J. A. Minich, 217–238. Durham: Duke University Press, 2023.

Kolářová, Kateřina. "Sesterství, navzdory: Radikální outsiderství Audre Lorde" [Sisterhood, regardless: The radical outsiderism of Audre Lorde]. Preface to *Sister Outsider: Eseje a projevy* [Sister Outsider: Essays and speeches], by Audre Lorde, 4–15. Translated by Markéta Musilová. Prague: tranzit.cz, 2021.

Kolářová, Kateřina, Tereza Stöckelová, and Lukáš Senft. "Disability and the (dysbiotic) gut: Sensing, tasting and knowing with food." *Sociology of Health & Illness* 45, no. 6 (July 2023): 1242–1258.

Kolářová, Kateřina, Lukáš Senft, and Tereza Stöckelová. "Sympoietic growth: living and producing with fungi in times of ecological distress." *Agriculture and Human Values* 40 (October 2023): 359–371.

Kateryna Lysovenko

Vienna, * Kyiv, Ukraine, 1989

Kateryna Lysovenko is studying post-conceptual art in the studio of professor Marina Gržinić at the Academy of Fine Arts Vienna. Her media are monumental painting, painting, drawing and text. Lysovenko is engaged in the study of the relationship between ideology and painting, the production of the image of the victim in politics and art, from antiquity to the present day. Lysovenko looks at painting as a language that can be instrumentalized or liberated.

Goodbye, East! Goodbye, Narcissus!, group exhibition, curated by Tanel Rander, EKKM, Tallin, Estonia, 2023

Kaleidoscope of (Hi)stories: Ukrainian Art 1913–2023, group exhibition, curated by Tatiana Kochubinskaya and Masha Isserlis, Albertinum, Staatliche Kunstsammlungen, Dresden, Germany, 2023

NORM, curated by Nikita Kadan, an apartment exhibition, Kyiv, Ukraine, 2023

Handle with Care, group exhibition, curated by Victoria Popovics and Kristina Szipőcs, Budapest, Hungary, 2023–2024

Kyiv Biennale in Vienna, curated by Hedwig Saxenhuber, Georg Schöllhammer, Sergey Klymko, Vienna, Austria, 2023

Freefilmers Mariupol, curated by Oksana Kazmina and Ivana Marjanović, Kunstraum Innsbruck, Austria, 2023–2024

Propaganda for the world of my dreams, curated by Tomáš Glanc, Universität Zürich, Switzerland, 2023

A Naked Room, curated by Lisa German and Maria Lanko, The Naked Room Gallery, Kyiv, Ukraine, 2023

Where Ruins Grow Like Plants or Child Body, curated by Antoni Burzyński, Krupa Gallery, Wrocław, Poland, 2024

Tomasz Rakowski

Warsaw, * Wrocław, Poland, 1974
Tomasz Rakowski is an ethnologist, cultural anthropologist, and associate professor at the Institute of Ethnology and Cultural Anthropology, University of Warsaw. He also lectures at the Institute of Polish Culture. His research interests include social art, phenomenological anthropology, post-socialist transformation, and post-socialist, bottom-up developments. He conducts field studies in Poland and Mongolia.

Rakowski, Tomasz. "Social deeds, building, and the cosmopolitan moment: an ethnographic view on affective labour in (late) socialist Poland." In *Cosmopolitan Moment, Cosmopolitan Method*, edited by Huon Wardle and Nigel Rapport, 138–155. London: Routledge, 2023.

Rakowski, Tomasz. "'Urbanisation of the Steppe': Sedentarization, Mobility, and Collective Business-Making Among the Torghuts in Post-transitional Mongolia." In "Urbanisation and Kinship in Inner Asia." Special issue, *Prace Etnograficzne* 49, no. 1–2 (2021): 1–20.

Rakowski, Tomasz. "Elements of the Country and the Space of the City: Artistic Experiments." In *The Rural: Documents of Contemporary Art*, 222–227. Cambridge, MA: The MIT Press, 2019.

Rakowski, Tomasz. *Hunters, Gatherers, and Practitioners of Powerlessness: An Ethnography of the Degraded in Postsocialist Poland.* Oxford: Berghahn Books, 2019.

Rakowski, Tomasz. "A Cultural Cyclotron: Ethnography, Art Experiments, and a Challenge of Moving Towards the Collaborative in Rural Poland." In *Experimental Collaborations: Ethnography Through Fieldwork Devices*, edited by Tomás Sánchez Criado and Adolfo Estalella, 154–178. Oxford: Berghahn Books, 2018.

Marta Romankiv

Krakow, * Lviv, Ukraine, 1995
Marta Romankiv (she/her) is an interdisciplinary artist who works with installations, video, and social situations. Romankiv graduated from the Lviv State College of Decorative and Applied Arts and the Academy of Art in Szczecin. She is currently completing her PhD at the Academy of Fine Arts in Gdańsk. Her practice is mostly focused on civil and workers' rights, social exclusion in the context of migration, and the identity issues associated with it. Most of her projects are participation-based, situated at the intersection of activism, the social sciences, and art. In 2021, she supported migrants from Ukraine in the process of establishing the first trade union of household workers in Poland.

I Dreamt About Europe, video, 5:00 min., Art Agenda Nova, KRAKERS (Krakow Art Week), Krakow, Poland, 2022

Euroworkshop, video installation, Pawilon, Poznań, Poland, 2022 / Museum of Warsaw, Poland, 2023

You Can Count On Me, social initiative, Warsaw, Poland, 2021–present

The Luncheon On The Grass, video in collaboration with the Domestic Workers Committee, 12:00 min., Warsaw, Poland, 2021

Where is the Monument of the Housemaid?, photo documentation, Bunkier Sztuki Gallery of Contemporary Art, Krakow, Poland, 2022

Immigrant, take a vote!, happening, Poznań, Szczecin, Gdańsk, Warsaw, and Białystok, Poland, 2020

Galina Rymbu
Lviv, * Omsk, Russia, 1990
Galina Rymbu is a poet and a modern poetry researcher. Rymbu was the original creator and curator of the feminist educational literary project Ф-письмо (F-Writing), and she also edited an online magazine of the same name. Together with Eugene Ostashevsky and Ansley Morse, she compiled the first anthology of Russophone feminist poetry in English: *F-Letter*. Rymbu also curated the Arkadii Dragomoshchenko Poetry Prize, and she is the founder and editor of the Russophone micro-media project on modern poetry ГРЁЗА (DREAM). Selected poems of hers have been published in *n+1*, *Granta*, *The White Review*, *Music & Literature*, *Asymptote*, *Новое литературное обозрение* (New literary review), and *Воздух* (Air), among other publications. Rymbu won the main prize of the literary festival Poetry Without Borders in Riga, Latvia, in 2017. Her book *Life in Space* was shortlisted for The Derek Walcott Prize in 2020.

Rymbu, Galina. *Life in Space*. New York: Ugly Duckling Presse, 2020.
Rymbu, Galina. *Ты—будущее* [You, the Future]. Moscow: Центрифуга, 2020.
Rymbu, Galina. *Время земли* [Time of the Ground]. Kharkiv: KNTXT, 2018.
Rymbu, Galina. *Передвижное пространство переворота* [The Movable Space of a Coup]. Moscow: Арго-риск, 2014.
Rymbu, Galina. *White Bread*. Kingston: After Hours LTD, 2016.

Olia Sosnovskaya
Vienna/Minsk, * Minsk, Belarus, 1988
Olia Sosnovskaya is an artist, writer, and cultural organizer. Intertwining performance with text-based and visual arts (video essays, digital collages), she focuses on the notions of festivity, collective choreographies, and the political. She is a member of the self-organized platform Work Hard! Play Hard! (with Dzina Zhuk, Aleksei Borisionok, and Nikolay Spesivtsev), which deals with work, leisure, and non-institutional infrastructures and knowledge. She is also a member of the artistic-research group Problem Collective (with Alesia Zhitkevich, Aleksei Borisionok, and Uladzimir Hramovich). She is currently a PhD in practice candidate at the Academy of Fine Arts Vienna with a research project on the 2020 anti-government uprising in Belarus, addressing forms of political organizing, protest choreographies, strikes, solidarity, and care networks, which she approaches through performative practices and movement scores. Her individual and collective works have been presented in galleries and institutions such as Tanzquartier (Vienna), Kunsthalle Wien Karlsplatz (Vienna), HAU (Berlin), Museum of Modern Art in Warsaw, Display (Prague), Mystetskyi Arsenal (Kyiv), the Kyiv Biennial, e-flux (New York), and Y Gallery (Minsk), among others.

Sosnovskaya, Olia. “The Poetics and Politics of Interruption in the 2020–21 Belarus Uprising.” In “Formations of Feminist Strike.” Special issue, *Atlantis: Critical Studies in Gender, Culture & Social Justice* 44, no. 2 (2023): 40–52.
Sosnovskaya, Olia, and G. “Apparently, exile is our home.” *Typography: Translocal Dialogues on Home, Migration and Solidarity*, 2023. https://typography-worldwide.org/en/2023/02/07/olia-g-eng/.
Sosnovskaya, Olia, Tatsiana Shchurko, Georgy Mamedov, Sujatha Subramanian, and Jennifer Suchland. “Geographies of Solidarity: Protests in Belarus through a Transnational Feminist

Perspective." *Feminist Translocalities*, 2023. https://feminisms.co/zine/ographies-of-solidarity#!/tab/539477302-2.

Sosnovskaya, Olia. "The Walk: On Gestures, Movements and Rhythms of the Current Resistance in Belarus." In *Danceolitics*, 147–163. Berlin: Uferstudios GmbH, 2021.

Sosnovskaya, Olia. "Future Perfect Continuous." *DING*, no. 3 (2020). dingdingding.org/issue-3/future-perfect-continuous/.

Alex Toshkov

Fes, * Sofia, Bulgaria, 1977

Alex Toshkov is a historian of East-Central Europe and the Balkans in the modern period. His work explores the articulation of a politicized peasant subjectivity in the period between the two World Wars and the attempt to elaborate an alternative, agrarian modernity between capitalism and communism. A professor at the Euromed University of Fes since 2021, he has taught historical, theoretical, and methodological courses in the faculties of L'Ecole Euro-Méditerranéenne d'Architecture, de Design et d'Urbanisme (EMADU), the Euromed Business School (EBS), L'Institut de Science Juridique et Politique (ISJP), and the Faculty of Social and Human Sciences (FSHS). He is the director of the Euromed Language Center, which is currently reimagining English instruction at the university based on leveled, inter-faculty groups.

Toshkov, Alex. *Agrarianism as Modernity in 20th-Century Europe: The Golden Age of the Peasantry*. New York: Bloomsbury Academic, 2019.

Toshkov, Alex. "Проблемът за корупцията в светлината на 'Делото Стамболийски'" [The problem of corruption in light of the "Stamboliiski process"]. In *Евразийски хоризонти: минало и настояще* [Eurasian horizons: Past and present], edited by M. Vekov, N. Poppetrov, A. Zapranova, P. Peykowska, and M. Malinova, 30–50. Sofia: Institute for Historical Research, BAS, 2011.

Tomáš Uhnák

Prague, * Bratislava, Czechoslovakia, 1984

Tomáš Uhnák received his master's degrees from the Academy of Fine Arts in Prague and from the food policy program at City, University of London. He is currently a PhD student at the Czech University of Life Sciences Prague, researching discursive, ideological, and material formations of agro-food paradigms, food regimes, alternative food networks, and theories of transformation. He is a member of the Association of Local Food Initiatives (AMPI), where his agenda involves community-supported agriculture, organic agriculture, food sovereignty, and agroecology. He contributes regularly to a number of Czech and international magazines and journals on the topics of the social aspects and political economy of food systems and agriculture. He is a fruit cultivator with a focus on heirloom fruit varieties. In his art performances he uses food as a political and social tool.

Uhnák, Tomáš. "Reclaiming the Commons, Sharing the Land: From Meta-Cooking to a Rose Bush Thorn Stuck in a Finger." In *Season Five: An Assortment of Contributions on Themes of Land, Art, and Commons*, 76–88. Berlin: Universität der Künste, 2018.

Uhnák, Tomáš, and M. P. Pimbert. "Agroecology and Food Sovereignty: Charting a Way to a Radical Transformation of the Food System." In *Politics of Food*, edited by Dani

Burrows and Aaron Cezar, 88–99. London: Sternberg Press and the Delfina Foundation, 2019.

Zagata, Lukáš, Tomáš Uhnák, and Jiří Hrabák. “Moderately Radical? Stakeholders’ Perspectives on Societal Roles and Transformative Potential of Organic Agriculture.” *Ecological Economics* 190 (December 2021).

Uhnák, Tomáš. “The Silent Desperation of Aquatic Slaves: The Social and Environmental Economics of the Fishing Industry.” In *Animal Touch*, edited by Eva Koťátková and Hana Janečková, 119–133. Prague: ArtMap, 2021.

Maja Vusilović

Brno, * Čakovec, Croatia, 1990

Maja Vusilović is a feminist activist, writer, and union organizer in the care sector. In 2022, they founded the feminist magazine *Druhá : směna* (Second Shift) with their comrades. They presently serve there as an editor alongside writer and activist Eliška Koldová. Their work revolves around materialist feminism, reproductive justice, migration and the pursuit of establishing a mass anti-capitalist feminist movement (not only) in the Czech Republic.

Vusilović, Maja. “A proto ti, moře, děkuji! Jak křehké jsou turistické kulisy Chorvatska?” [And therefore, sea, thank you! How fragile is the tourist scenery of Croatia?]. *Druhá : směna.* Accessed May 17, 2024. https://druhasmena.cz/clanky/a-proto-ti-more-dekuji.

Vusilović, Maja. “Z války si nic nepamatuji” [I don’t remember anything from the war]. *Tvar*, no. 11 (May 2022). https://itvar.cz/z-valky-si-nic-nepamatuji.

Vusilović, Maja. “Totálně vyčerpaná? Sebevykořisťování jako obranný mechanismus v pozdním kapitalismu” [Totally exhausted? Self-exploitation as a defense mechanism in late capitalism]. *Druhá : směna.* Accessed May 17, 2024. https://druhasmena.cz/clanky/totalne-vycerpana.

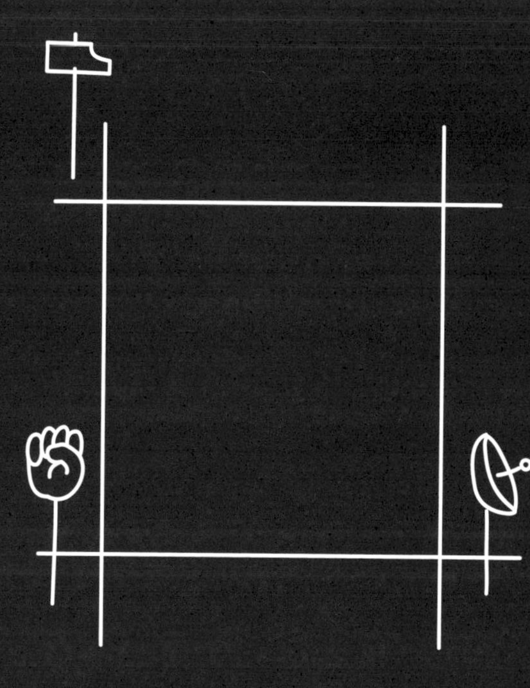

Sowing Unrest

Co-published by
tranzit.cz and Spector Books on the occasion of the Biennale Matter of Art 2024, Prague.

Editors
Aleksei Borisionok,
Katalin Erdődi

Managing Editor
Karin Akai

Texts
Kateryna Aliinyk, Aleksei Borisionok, Ramona Duminicioiu, Katalin Erdődi, Fernando García-Dory, Kateřina Kolářová, Tomasz Rakowski, Marta Romankiv, Galina Rymbu, Olia Sosnovskaya, Alex Toshkov, Tomáš Uhnák, Maja Vusilović

Visual Essays
Orla Barry, eeefff,
Kateryna Lysovenko,
Tamás Kaszás

Proofreading
and Copyediting
Ashley Davis,
Brian D. Vondrak

Translations
Joan Brooks,
Yustyna Kravchuk,
Inga Michalewska

Design
The Rodina

Typeface
Lars Pro by Bold Decisions

Printing
and Binding
Tiskárny Havlíčkův Brod, a.s.

ISBN
978-80-87259-60-3
978-3-95905-865-0
(Spector Books)

Spector Books
Harkortstraße 10
04107 Leipzig
Germany
www.spectorbooks.com

Distribution
GERMANY, AUSTRIA
GVA, Gemeinsame Verlagsauslieferung Göttingen GmbH&Co. KG,
www.gva-verlage.de

SWITZERLAND
AVA Verlagsauslieferung AG,
www.ava.ch

FRANCE, BELGIUM
Interart Paris,
www.interart.fr

UK
Central Books Ltd,
www.centralbooks.com

NORTH AND SOUTH AMERICA, AFRICA
ARTBOOK / D.A.P.,
www.artbook.com

SOUTH KOREA
The Book Society,
www.thebooksociety.org

JAPAN
twelvebooks,
www.twelve-books.com

AUSTRALIA, NEW ZEALAND
Perimeter Distribution,
perimeterdistribution.com

tranzit.cz
Dittrichova 337/13
120 00 Prague
CZ

matterof.art
tranzit.org

This book was published with the support of the Ministry of Culture of the Czech Republic.

tranzit is an initiative in the field of contemporary art. Its main partner is ERSTE Foundation.

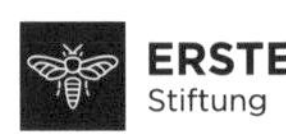

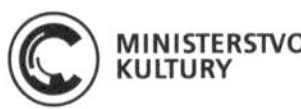

tranzit.cz